Y0-EBC-435

Straight Talk

Voices from the new South Africa

Dawin Meckel
Ole Keune

First published in 2004 by Struik Publishers
(a division of New Holland Publishing (South Africa) (Pty) Ltd)
New Holland Publishing is a member of Johnnic Communications Ltd
Log on to our photographic website www.imagesofafrica.co.za

Garfield House, 86–88 Edgware Road, London W2 2EA, United Kingdom
80 McKenzie Street, Cape Town 8001, South Africa
14 Aquatic Drive, Frenchs Forest, NSW 2086, Australia
218 Lake Road, Northcote, Auckland, New Zealand

ISBN 1 77007 008 7
10 9 8 7 6 5 4 3 2 1

Publishing manager: Dominique le Roux
Managing editor: Lesley Hay-Whitton
Proofreader: Erika Bornman
Translators: Mercedes Hanel and Erika Bornman

Reproduction by Hirt & Carter Cape (Pty) Ltd
Printed and bound by Sing Cheong Printing Company Limited

Thank you to all the people in the book for sharing your experiences with us. We tried our best to remain faithful to your stories :: Brandon Wood for not hating us :: Fanuel Motsepe for sharing house, pool and nunus :: Gray Robertson, Yvette Geyer, Nicole Brown, Anastasia White and Celesté Holmes for sharing your address books :: Clayton Wakefort, NN Isaacs, Bruce, Bertie and friends, Paul Pather and family, Hazel Shelton, John Hastings and Kaizer Ngwenya for broadening our South African horizon :: Gerd Fleischmann and Wim Boes for your advice :: Barbara Goll for reading it all :: Nicole Welgen for inspiration, patience and optimism :: Our friends and families for being there :: You are because of others

Dawin Meckel and Ole Keune – Introduction 14
Thando Sekame – participated in the 1976 student uprising against Afrikaans. 22
Mbongeni Mzola – teaches in a school on the Eastern Cape coast. 30
Jerome – is travelling through South Africa in a camper van with his girlfriend and friends. 34
Wiehan – puts the blame for the high crime rate at the door of people of colour. 42
Vicky Yokwana – heads up a garden project in Guguletu township in Cape Town. 46
Avril Hoepner – a social worker who cares for homeless and blind people. 52
Sophia Loum – runs the Sothemba organisation that cares for HIV-infected people. 56
Kyle, Nicholas, Daniel and Ali – young BMX riders in Bellville, Cape Town. 64
Alfred Gürtel – grew up in Namibia and has retired to a German old age home in South Africa. 74
Ready D – DJ and producer of Universal Souljaz, one of South Africa's first hip-hop bands. 82
Henry – grew up in District Six, but his family was forcibly removed to the Cape Flats. 92
Anthony Booysen – spent sixteen years in Pollsmoor prison for armed robbery. 96
Letepe Maisela – Managing Director and founder of two companies in Johannesburg. 104
Nkhensani Manganyi – founded the Stoned Cherrie fashion label based in Johannesburg. 112
Vanessa Raphaely – Editorial Director of Associated Magazines, which publishes *Cosmopolitan*. 114
Fanuel Motsepe – a Johannesburg-based architect born to a Tswana royal family. 124
Motamane Mathosi – founder of Mathosi Engineering Services, is proud of his dreadlocks. 130
Millicent Maroga – has won a Nelson Mandela scholarship to Manchester University. 134
Leslie Kasumbu – DJ at Yfm Radio in Johannesburg, was born in Uganda. 138
Sindile Mvambi – a township tour guide, one of the few black people to attend a white school. 144
Nadine Naidoo – singer, soap opera star, presenter of a TV show and founder of VIA Africa. 148

MEX
PLAY CANYON
McDonald's
KFC
CONES
1.95
SCOPE

"The moment for which I had waited so long came and I folded my ballot paper and cast my vote. It was like falling in love. The sky looked blue and more beautiful. I saw the people in a new light. They were beautiful, they were transfigured. I too was transfigured. It was dreamlike. You were scared someone would rouse you and you would awake to the nightmare that was apartheid's harsh reality." Archbishop Desmond Tutu, Nobel Peace Prize winner (*No Future without Forgiveness*)

You go all the way down Long Street, through Cape Town's city centre, past all the colourful little shops. You enjoy the sun and the feeling of meeting so many very different people going about their daily lives in harmony. Unlike all-too-grey Germany, where everybody is chasing the clock, life here seems so carefree. On the street, people look one another in the eye, greeting from time to time, just like that, even though they have probably never met before.

You sit down in a coffee shop. This is something you do quite often, because coffee is cheap here, much cheaper than back home in Germany. When you're paying, you notice a child outside, who just at that moment is bringing his fist to his mouth to take a hit from his glue packet. He looks directly at the money that you have just taken from your pocket and put on the table. Seven rand. Not much really – converted into Euros, about 70 cents. His gaze remains glued to your money for just a short while, though for you it is long enough to read his thoughts – or you think you can. You imagine yourself mirrored in his eyes. You see yourself sitting there. Behind the glass pane. The one that protects you not only from the noise and dust of the street, but also from various unpleasantnesses. Like the caged bear at the zoo that gets stones thrown at him through the bars by badly brought-up little brats. Only this time it's the other way round.

You feel bad or – far worse – trapped. Trapped again by your attempt to lead a completely normal life – 'normal', that is, according to prosperous middle-class European standards. You sit in one of those trendy places, with the cool waitrons and the even cooler wall hangings. Nothing special and definitely nothing bad. But, even so, at that moment you feel bad, betrayed, overlooked. Like a prosperous middle-class European removed from the limelight. Perhaps not for long, but at least for a short while, you once again sense that strange feeling in your stomach. One of those moments that you often experience here and to which you are slowly but surely becoming accustomed.

You feel guilty. But for what? Because you paid seven rand for a cup of coffee? Money that that poor kid outside could desperately have used. Why did the little guy have to show up just at this moment?

With the loss of your identity and your feeling of self-worth, you will still somehow learn to get by. In any case things are getting better day by day. You must simply sort yourself out again. Know where you stand, here, where the First and so-called Third Worlds seem to melt together. In principle you are one of those who believe that through humanity and brotherliness the world can still be saved. One of those who always have some small change in their pocket to give to the needy on the street. And, yes, one of those who are pleased that the safety gate at the front door of their house was installed sooner than expected. But you're certainly completely different from the all-too-rich whites in Camps Bay where bright white villas, guarded by electronic security systems and vicious dogs, are surrounded by high concrete walls, keeping views of reality at bay. No, really, you are not like them. So you certainly don't need to have a guilty conscience because of a cup of coffee. In any case, things are going much better for the majority of the population. Better than before. Before, there was apartheid; today everybody is equal. On paper anyway. Sure, there are still differences. Differences that one can't iron out so quickly. It isn't that long ago that the siren would sound at seven in the evening and blacks would all have to vacate the city centre. They would have to go back, but back to where? To the outlying areas, the townships. And, still today, the only contact that you as a white person are forced to have with these areas is when you're using the N2 highway in the direction of the airport.

It's a while now since we – excited, curious and a little apprehensive – embarked on our twenty-minute taxi ride between Cape Town airport and the city centre. It was warm, as is Africa, and everything was running very smoothly. The airport had been up to Western standards and the taxi driver had obligingly helped with the big rucksacks. The corners of our mouths no longer turned down and our good moods could not be concealed. The same could be said for the taxi driver who had dark skin and happily told us, with a rolling 'r' and remarkable accent, where he came from and asked how long our holiday was to be.

We had explained that we were not here just for fun. We were no average tourists. Rather, we told him – not without a little pride – we planned to stay for six months to complete our foreign semester at our sister school of photography and graphics in Cape Town. A mere five-minute drive later and everything had changed. Townships. Shacks were everywhere. When you've been in Africa for five minutes, racing past ten minutes of endless, uninhabitable decayed-looking corrugated iron shacks is more than sobering. There were thousands of them, kept back from the road by fences. Naturally, we had read about the townships, and maybe even seen a TV documentary report about them, but the actual live view was shocking.

And yet it seems that, just behind these fences, the pulse of life is beating much faster. The streets are full of people, animals, dust and stands where you can buy anything from a sheep's head to a pocket calculator disguised as a cell phone. Impressions rain down on you at high speed. You don't feel comfortable. You are an intruder and you know all the stories. You have heard of the high crime rate and that as a white person you must be very careful. The travel guidebook advises that you avoid these areas completely. One more reason for you to form your own opinion, you think.

The people living there today used to live on the land; or at least, their ancestors did. They tried to flee the poor conditions of the homelands, where blacks where forced to live, and hoped to find work in the city. Outside their homelands their movement was restricted: they had to carry 'pass' books and lived in fear of arrest. By creating these pseudo independent islands within South Africa's borders, the apartheid regime gave blacks the status of foreigners. They could visit the city as cheap labour during the day, but by nightfall had to be back in the townships, where they lived in sheet metal shacks.

'If you came to town to visit your husband, who was working here for a year, the government arrested you and put you in jail, because you were not legal here in the Western Cape. You were illegal.' [Vicky Yokwana, page 46]

With the loss of identity went the loss of tradition. 'We are trying to bring it back. There were a lot of people who wanted to be Westernised; they called it Western civilisation. They learned to forget their tradition. Arts and Culture is there to bring back those sweet memories about who you are. People must know themselves.' [Mbongeni Mzola, page 31] People live here in the smallest space imaginable, squeezed next to each other. There are areas with unemployment figures of up to ninety percent. So what must you do when you do not even have enough money to feed your family? When you live from hand to mouth? You cannot expect any social grants from the government. You simply do not know what tomorrow will bring. It's really simple: don't give up hope. Try, somehow, to survive. Some go from door to door, offering to neaten the garden, or they learn to grow their own vegetables and so have a full stomach and find inner peace. 'So we built up this community garden with the help of the Presbyterian Church. Seventy-two people can share this garden. Each of them can have a small plot. Besides the gardening skills, we also train them in other skills, like peace skills. People, when they are hungry, they are angry. There is no peace, there is nothing and they get sick.' [Vicky Yokwana]

Much has changed since 1994, even for families who live in small shacks in District Six in which, in wintertime, the water lies knee-deep. They were afraid that the new government could, at any time, come again with bulldozers to drive them away. The land on which they were born, on which they grew up, does not belong to them. Their fears proved to be unfounded. The government did come back, in 2004, and the shacks were again demolished. But, this time, real houses were put up for the inhabitants. They could just move in.

These people did not allow themselves to be driven away when, in 1968, the bulldozers first came to flatten their houses and level out the earth in this quarter of the city. This process continued for years, because, according to the white government, the coloured people there were living too close to the city centre. Sixty thousand people were evicted strictly according to the colour of their skin – a symbol of the desperation of the regime of the time to end the co-habitation of people of different races and skin colours. Freed black slaves, Indian and Malaysian traders, artists and also workers and immigrants from all over the world had settled here peacefully to create the functional, multi-cultural quarter known as District Six. Now those people were shipped into the townships and friends, families and acquaintances were torn apart. 'District Six was a very musical community. I would say it was musically driven. My father, my family, my ancestors, that's definitely where it all started for me. People were situated and split. A lot of District Six people were all split up. The people came from all different areas and thrown into Mitchell's Plain as neighbours.' [Ready D, page 84]

The perception is that Johannesburg's city centre is unsafe for whites, particularly tourists. This is certainly what you are led to believe on arrival at the bus terminus. You are asked why on earth you would want to endanger yourselves. What could be your motivation? But your purpose is simple enough: to capture the multitude of visual impressions, and the pace and fundamental dynamism of an African city evolving daily. This evolution is more keenly observed and experienced in Johannesburg than the relative conservatism of Cape Town. In Jo'burg, a place where whites are clearly in the minority, your experience turns out to be completely the opposite of the 'not safe for a second' mindset so prevalent among a class that has fallen from grace.

After 1994, Sandton experienced a developmental boom, with many businesses relocating from the city centre to the northern suburbs: a new island of gleaming prosperity, at a safe distance from the perceived growing instability of the inner city. Nobody finds themselves in Sandton without a reason: you are either a wealthy South African or a tourist contributing to economic growth in a labyrinthine mall designed to induce frivolous spending. You are made to feel at home by the adoption of knee-jerk European 'style'. While the super-rich while away the hours in faux-Parisian cafés, the real cooking occurs in the melting-pot that is Jo'burg proper. Stalls – semi-formal businesses – are ubiquitous. Fruit and vegetables, cigarettes, shoes – the consumer's needs are comprehensively catered for. In between all that, there are black and white businessmen hurrying from one meeting to another, wishing their day had twenty-five hours. During lunch hour you have to navigate physically through a sea of people. The collective energy driving the 'City of Gold' becomes palpable. Opportunities abound, and are seized as quickly as they present themselves. 'They have opportunities to start their own businesses, which is what's happening. Everybody is doing hundreds of things. Everybody is trying to make their mark and I think the youth is going to make South Africa a world power.' [Leslie Kasumbu, page 138] A revived black consciousness has found expression in fashion, music and literature. People are proud of their heritage, and are enthusiastically expressing this. 'Basically the idea was to find a way to reintroduce our history to people so that it is part of popular culture, through celebrating people who brought us here, like Steve Biko. But doing it in a way that speaks to young people.' [Nkhensani Manganyi, page 112] One can't change the past, but can forge the future in such a way that it is inclusively South African – where one's skin colour and belief system contribute to one's sense of national identity, instead of conflicting with it. The 1976 uprising was certainly not in vain; but, given a ten-year context for a fledgling democracy, it is possible that we need a few decades more. 'We need the economy to grow and we want people to start sharing in the economy. So it is a very tough act, for government, for the corporate world, for us.' [Letepe Maisela, page 104]

After spending two months at City Varsity in Cape Town in 2001, we decided not to continue with our studies, but through photo-journalism rather to try to gain our own insight into this country as it stands today, after a decade of democracy. *Straight Talk* was intended as a vehicle to allow people from the most diverse echelons of South African society to speak, and in their own words to give their impressions of the lay of this land. Dawin Meckel and Ole Keune

I was in that first group of kids of 1976 that actually rose up against the introduction of Afrikaans as a medium of education. We are now known as the lost generation.

Many East Germans and many West Germans, after the wall came down, or even while it was up, wanted to know what was on the other side, and occasionally people escaped from that side, to bring the stories back. In South Africa it was a bit different, because when our wall was coming down – a wall similar to your wall, but a wall of apartheid – there was not the same type of enthusiasm; there was more fear. Security was built up, as you can see. If you look in our cities, you can see the high police presence and you can see all these private security companies. I have to show you so many comparisons between your country and ours, because that is really important.

Where we failed, where you people have been successful, was when your wall came down you had that inspiration of going to see what's going on on the other side of the wall. As a result you can see the disparities between East and West. And the West took on the initiative by paying a tax known as *Solidarität*, which actually assisted the growth, so that the imbalance could be adjusted. That hasn't occurred here. By introducing that tax of *Solidarität* you were actually safeguarding yourself against future instability. Although people in the West might feel it is a burden, it's better to have that type of burden than people coming later and have civil unrest. I mean you're going through unification and that's a nice way of repairing. It is what has happened in communist countries. It wasn't the same as it is here in South Africa.

The Berlin wall coming down played a significant role in our democracy. Are you aware of that? Our struggle was tainted with communism. With elimination of the Cold War, the communists were no longer a threat and, as a result, we were no longer a threat, as the South African government had perceived us to be.

So on the 9th of November [1989] when your wall came down, our life changed. Two months later Mandela was a free man and five years later we entered a new democracy. The situation that you see now is basically what you would have seen in Germany in 1919 when the League of Nations humiliated Germany and made it less of a country. And as a result you people have actually seen how France in the Ruhr/Rhein area took up iron and used it for the benefit of France, to the annoyance of the average German

< **Thando Sekame** (38) lives in Guguletu, Cape Town. In his opinion, Germany's history has very close ties with that of his country.

<< On the way to Thando's home (pages 20–21).

Reconciliation means, if a person reaches out his hand, grip it. You can't take just the little finger.

person. There were even minority groups that were enriching themselves at the expense of the German people. By 1929 you had what was called the world depression which affected the German people. And it took just one nut guy to come and see the situation and read the public sentiment. He spoke on the sentiments and people stood up collectively and they were called Nazis.

So by 1933 we get the introduction of the Nazi party. And people didn't denounce this, even though they were a minority party in the beginning. And through those events you have actually restored your dignity. But today nobody treats you as scum any more. You are now a recognised person and not a bad one. Why? Because you stood up against that.

In South Africa, we had the white liberals, intellectuals, who started a communist party. And the communist movement during the earlier years was a workers' struggle. As a result of the fact that many blacks were workers, the Communist Party identified with the Black Nationalist movements. That led to a sort of coalition between the two. And then later those white liberals belonging to the Communist Party could raise their voice on the workers' issues which were basically black issues, because blacks couldn't speak for themselves. The white Afrikaners, who were very Calvinistic, were afraid of these communists for their very existence, which means Christianity, because that was the biggest fear that the old white Afrikaner government instilled in the white community: that communism means the absence of religious freedom.

Now we have a democracy. On paper we are equal. Economically we are not. We also carry a legacy or an inheritance with us, which leads to unemployment, which leads to poverty, which leads to having a very low esteem of ourselves, while living under these conditions. A country where you don't have a home or land. Isn't that a recipe for war? In our new-found democracy, security has been built up. Not the army or the police. New security firms have mushroomed throughout South Africa. Dealing with the fear of thirteen percent of the population.

Reconciliation means, if a person reaches out his hand, grip it. You can't take just the little finger. And, if you know he is gonna tumble, you should grab him, because we share the same home, South Africa. But, because we have been tainted with fear over the years, apartheid means ignorance; apartheid means that we stay separated from each other. By being separated from each other, we became ignorant of each other. Ignorance is a big fear. And it is that court of fear that hasn't been surveyed here, because we had been conditioned for so many years.

Now we are told to forget the past and to move on. Yeah, we could have moved on, if we could have got on your back and guided you to get strong. But you're telling me to move on but you're sprinting off and I'm sitting here, and you're telling me, 'Oh, you don't want to stand up!' How can I stand up being crippled, if I believe in liberation before education? Have I liberated my country? Have I sacrificed my school years? My youth? So, when other people tell you to pluck the fruit of liberation, it is not fair. As I said, we speak about reconciliation. It is there. It is really, really important. But we can only reconcile if the person on the other side accepts my hand.

I was in that first group of kids of 1976 that actually rose up against the introduction of Afrikaans as a medium of education. All our subjects were given in Afrikaans, and that is what we could not understand. It's not that you were just being taught Afrikaans. No, all your subjects were in that language.

We are now known as the lost generation. Our maxim was 'liberation before education'. We burned down places, schools: our schools, where we were studying. The Bantu Education [the schooling that black people received] was just to make you an infant or a worker. Burning down a school benefited us, because new things were brought in. Things they could have bought in the beginning. Gates. There have never been gates or windows before. Suddenly, they had windows, when we burned down these places. Instead of sitting outside or sitting on the floor, now benches were brought in, because we have burned these places down. They also got fire hoses for the first time.

Thando Sekame ::

^ Thando's neighbourhood, Guguletu, Cape Town.

> A school in Coffee Bay on the Eastern Cape's Wild Coast, part of the former homeland of Transkei.

<< Many children in rural areas have to walk long distances to and from school each day (pages 26–27).

We hope that our learners will be people who will not be the job seekers. They will employ others.

< **Mbongeni Mzola** (33) is a teacher in a Coffee Bay school. This photo was taken in one of his classes.

We are using traditional methods of doing things. There are eight learning areas, and they include some of the traditional subjects. For instance Arts and Culture has been introduced, and Life Organisation has been introduced. They have been brought in to make people aware of diseases like HIV/Aids.

Our own art and culture was marginalised in previous years, because of the segregation or discrimination of our people. Back in time we became urbanised. We lost our identity. We also lost our roots; we didn't go back to our roots. But now, since we are free, we did go to our roots. We are trying to bring it back. There were a lot of people who wanted to be Westernised; they called it Western civilisation. They learned to forget their tradition. Arts and Culture is there to bring back those sweet memories about who you are. People must know themselves.

Even if you go to certain occasions today, people are not wearing Western clothes; they wear their traditional clothes. That thing alone was our morality, and it also showed our identity. We are able to identify ourselves. But before that we were unable, because we were a little bit confused because of that Western civilisation.

What happened was we were taken from our rural areas to mines in urban areas, especially those people who were uneducated or illiterate. They were taken to the mines to dig for gold and platinum and diamonds, and then after twelve months you go home, and after three months you had to go back again. Migrant labour alone made us lose our identity, because of poverty, hunger, murder and things like that. But today we hope we are having a light on top of the mountain.

Today we have technologies, for instance, in our learning areas. Technology! That technology was not introduced to us before 1994, but today we have technology at our schools. Even the poorest of the poor use technology. They learn how to use it in school. They learn technology. This was something we didn't dream about before. Those are the things that make us feel proud.

We hope that our learners in 2005 will be people who will not be the job seekers. They will employ others.

Mbongeni Mzola ::

> Coffee Bay children playing on the beach after a day at school.

INKOMAZI
MAAS

I first went to a coloured school and there they called me Spook – it means 'ghost' – because I was white compared to them.

My mother is coloured and from Durban. She met my father in 1971. He's white and they couldn't get married. My little brother was born in 1981. They lived against the rules for ten years. They lived together – like on and off – in the underground or under false identity. They did it, like, nothing ever happened – a lot of people did it. I'm the result of it.

Apartheid was weird. When I was young, it didn't click so much. There was a separation for me during my life, because I had to be one person with my friends and another person with my family at home on the weekends. I couldn't tell my white friends where my coloured cousins lived, for example. Apartheid was quite shit in that way. The other kids also, they noticed that you are not exactly the same but it didn't really bother most of them. Sometimes you got teased. I first went to a coloured school and there they called me Spook – it means 'ghost' – because I was white compared to them. And, when you went to a white school, you weren't exactly white; you didn't have straight hair, so you had another name. But I did not really suffer from it. Not that much.

The break of apartheid wasn't just one break. I know that in '81 my mother and my father could get married. So there was a break then already, but apartheid wasn't finished. But you must remember that even today people still have stereotypes in their head, like black people steal and Afrikaners got hard heads, not so intelligent and very set in their ways. They also have got very good people, the majority of them, you know. They originally came here for freedom, for a better opportunity to live with nature, and they did a lot for this country, a lot. They built it up. But a lot of destruction also goes with the building.

In one way I'm disappointed with the ANC government, because we had a chance to really make things right. We had a chance for a new government, new ideas, new ways forward, you know. The protection of the land – really good things we could have done. Now they are adopting the Western system. We are paying American crime specialists to tell us how to deal with crime. America's got the highest crime rate in the world and we are paying them millions of dollars. We have been in war for twenty years in this country and now for the first time we are not in war and they want to go and spend sixty billion rand on weapons. Fifty million people living in this country. With sixty billion you could build each person a house or two houses worth a million rand and buy them a car and a cow. Everybody would be sorted out. It just doesn't make sense. Our government is as corrupt as any other and nothing has changed. The power has just shifted from one hand to another, that's what I believe. It might sound racist, but black people are not experienced in politics. They had lower education. When they got introduced to politics, they got introduced to Western politics. It's a system of slavery, if you know what I mean. We had the chance then to make it and have a really good system, different from everybody else.

For example, marijuana should be legalised in this country. African people have smoked it for thousands of years and it was made illegal here by the white people. If you were white and smoked it before, you had a hard time. The cops made sure it was a black person's thing. The ANC government is still making it illegal. But it has been proven that some of the people in the ANC government, their parents sold marijuana and sent them to university with the money they made from it. And the people make more money out of marijuana than sugar-cane. And sugar-cane for example has destroyed all the Natal coast in Zululand.

Jerome ::

< **Jerome** (26) is travelling through South Africa in a camper van with his girlfriend, their child and four friends.

> Leonsdale, a coloured area situated on the Cape Flats.

>> **Veranshia Coetzee** (18) with her friend **Stanford Wales** (32). Her daughter's father is in prison at the moment. She lives in Leonsdale (pages 38–39).

HOU ONS
OMGEWING
SKOON !!

adidas

^ **Frank** (30) burning off plastic insulation from telephone cables in the concrete settlement the Ranch on the Cape Flats. He is paid one hundred rand for twelve kilograms of wire.

I hate blacks and I love whites. If you walk through Cape Town you gonna see there is always a fucking kaffir walking with a white chick.

I do the quarter-mile in 9.45 seconds. We build up normal cars and we have races on public streets in town. We block the streets off and we race till the police come and split us apart. It's like, um, drive or get caught. It's an illegal street race. It's illegal but it's fun breaking the law. My buddy does the quarter-mile in 9.25 seconds. He's a little bit faster than me.

I use a V6 Golf with a totally modified engine. The whole car costs me, actually my uncle, about R650000. The *kak* [shit] costs a lot of money, but it's fun. Don't smash your car up, because it costs a lot.

I hate blacks and I love whites. If you walk through Cape Town you gonna see there is always a fucking kaffir walking with a white chick. You see it in the movies, the beautiful white chick is sleeping with that black guy. I hate this all.

I grew up with people like the AWB [Afrikaner Weerstandsbeweging, a right-wing organisation]. They are against coloureds. We are not like normal South Africans and we are not like the AWB. We are totally different. We are on our own.

When you get *kak* by them, we sort it out by ourselves, we don't run to the cops. When we see that someone else is in trouble, we stand up against these coloureds, we are not afraid of them. We are in a group of about sixty people. We are not actually violent, we are just minding our own business, but if we see that someone else is in trouble, or like that… Well, mostly these groups are walking around at night. Like weekends, when we see people going to clubs, you always find people around who want to steal their money. Then we are there to help the man who gets robbed. We are just getting rid of that other guy who tried to rob him. It's like a business we don't get paid for. It's just for the safety and to get the *kak* out of South Africa.

> **Wiehan** (24) lives on a housing estate in one of Cape Town's northern suburbs.

Maybe you are walking in Bellville and we are walking on the other side of the road and we see that there are two or three guys trying to rob you. We are not standing on the other side thinking, 'Oh, shit, what is that *kak*?' No, we come and help you and we don't even ask questions. We will take you away and we will sort him out. You won't see what we are doing to him. We won't kill him. He just won't rob you any more. I will let them bite the pavement…

A few years ago, everywhere they told you, Cape Town is a very beautiful place. It was top in tourism. Everybody

Mandela was our first black president. He was the best president South Africa ever had. He was the best president.

right across the world came to Cape Town. This is the Mother City. But now, in books, in every newspaper, you read about tourism: people don't want to come to South Africa any more, because of gangsterism, drug fights and gang fights, taxi fights. The first thing we must do is take out all the fucking taxis and South Africa will be a better place. Because every second day you hear about them shooting one another.

There are a lot of coloured people here in South Africa that are against violence. I don't have a problem with them. But then you got these fucking arseholes that are too lazy to work. They just like to rob people. Like my other buddy was killed three months ago for his shoelace.

Do you use any signs? No, we don't use any signs. If you put on an AWB or a Nazi sign and maybe you beat up one guy, he will see the sign on you, he will recognise your face. He can easily point you out, because you got a mark on you. If you got a mark on you, you belong to a group and group violence, gangs in this place are very popular.

I don't belong to a gang. We are just a normal bunch of guys who stand up against gangsterism and all that shit that is going on.

South Africa was a very beautiful place, but now you see garbage everywhere and plastic bags. That's why we have that group. We are sorting that *kak* out. Last weekend, we were walking around with black bags and a lot of guys; we just started cleaning up this area. But not just cleaning up. If people have problems, they can come to me. Like, another guy was smoking dope. His one lung collapsed. They didn't call anybody else. They came to me, to come and help the guy. The guy died in my arms, his body was too weak. Jesus, this guy was like full of dope. Not actually dope, but buttons [mandrax]. I was staying with him, the cops came, the ambulance came, and took him out. When they asked me what happened, I told them. But I didn't tell them exactly the truth, because I cover up for some people. Because here, in this suburb, if something happens like that in a flat, you can't say, 'Ja, I was smoking weed [marijuana] with that person.' Because if you do that, they gonna lose that flat. And most people that stay here are, like, very old people, and young people stay here also, mostly married couples. And if you tell them, 'Listen, this guy was smoking weed with that guy,' they gonna lose their apartment and they gonna be on the street. The flats here are going for about three hundred to four hundred rand, for just the right size of the pocket. So they can survive for the month or the week. It's all about survival here.

Like Mandela, I know him. I met him before. On Robben Island. We were building that new harbour on Robben Island. I did all that steel work. I was working for underwater construction. We were living in containers, in steel boxes on the island. I stayed there for about six months. Me and Mandela were standing like you and me. He was our first black president. He was the best president South Africa ever had. He was the best president. He is not a president any more, but he is still doing good stuff for South Africa.
Wiehan ::

^ **Ethel Carstens** (83) and **Susie Evans** (64) live in the same area as Wiehan.

People were fighting outside, but they wouldn't fight here. I trained them in making peace. To make peace, they must have peace inside themselves.

During apartheid people were removed from their places. They were thrown out of town into the homelands, where there were no jobs. Women were separated from their husbands. If you came to town to visit your husband, who was working here for a year, the government arrested you and put you in jail, because you were not legal here in the Western Cape. You were illegal. No matter if you were a pregnant woman, or you got babies, you just ended up staying in jail. So people were suffering a lot.

The last government was bad to us. I was moved to Khayelitsha [the biggest township in Cape Town], where people were far away from town, from the shops. They were not working, they were hungry. We started this agriculture project in 1998. We started in backyard gardens, to visit each and every body, to talk about the land they had. We trained them and we gave them gardening skills. That was okay, because people were eating now. But there are people who have no formal houses, who are staying in shacks, who have got no yard, nothing. So people were sitting around, they were not doing anything. They were helpless and they had nothing in their pot to eat.

So we built up this community garden with the help of the Presbyterian Church. Seventy-two people can share this garden. Each of them can have a small plot. Besides the gardening skills, we also train them in other skills, like peace skills. People, when they are hungry, they are angry. There is no peace, there is nothing and they get sick.

In 1999 there was political fighting within the community. Members of one party were fighting against members of another party. All those people were coming here to me. So I had to solve their problems. They were fighting outside, but they wouldn't fight here. I trained them in making peace. To make peace, they must have peace inside themselves. I trained them to get peace inside themselves by doing the gardening workshops.

Here you can find people who are sick – like one of the ladies here. When she came here, she was very ill and she was so thin. We helped her do the garden. Now she is training the other people. She is healthy, she is doing the training herself. Now I'm working all around with her, training other people. I also train people who are HIV-positive. They eat healthy food and they have something to do now. And I got three requests to start new gardens for HIV-positive people. The co-ordinators of the clinics came to me. Here in the Western Cape there is a lot of TB and HIV. So we work together with people that have nothing, nothing.

We are working hand-in-hand with the police. Before, the police was depending on the government. Now we changed that attitude. So that they must work with the people. Before they were very rude. But now, when you come and ask for something, they treat you good. They are no more enemies.

How do you tell people to stay calm and not to fight? Like doing the three-day gardening courses. First of all I'm doing it theoretically, so that they can feel the peace inside, by talking, by doing the workshops, by asking them, 'How do you feel peace?' and they will just brainstorm. Then you put a paper on the wall and you put them in groups and you gonna talk about this. Then we tell them how to do the gardening theoretically. After that, they get a piece of land and I show them how to do it practically. And by working in the garden, watching their veggies grow, they get peaceful.

Vicky Yokwana ::

> **Vicky Yokwana** (55) (on the left) heads up a garden project in Guguletu township in Cape Town.

KWATHUNG APHA
27

151
153

INJAMA-IKHONA
143

^ Houses erected in Dunoon near Cape Town by the African National Congress government during the Reconstruction and Development Programme.

^ These people operate a shebeen (informal bar) in their house in Joza township, Grahamstown.

You know, if you grew up in a white suburb, like we did, you'd see black people stepping off the pavement when they approached you, and they never looked into your face.

> **Avril Hoepner** (48) is a social worker who cares for homeless and blind people.

I became a women's-activist before I became an anti-apartheid activist, working against apartheid. My husband Lawrence, a teacher, was more involved in the struggle than I was. He taught at a so-called coloured school in those days in Manenberg [Cape Town]. It's one of those areas where a lot of gang-related issues were happening. He supported the students, to ensure that they got their education. We were striving for a different South Africa, and how our struggle began, really, was to acknowledge the fact that, first of all, children were taught differently according to their race.

To be white and to come up against authorities was quite difficult, because you were immediately a target. A white person as a minority would stand out much more obviously in a demonstration than a group of black people.

Lawrence started to speak out against apartheid at mass meetings, wherever he was invited, even at church meetings. He started talking in schools during the student uprising in 1976. He tried to encourage people to consider what was going on in the disadvantaged communities. He was strong and vocal during that time. When he stood up, he just said what he had to say. At that time you couldn't do anything on your own. You must remember that there was a blanket on the freedom of press. You couldn't say what you thought. Even our own families rejected us, so that we had to struggle on our own. You couldn't watch movies, for argument's sake; the government cut out all the sex scenes. You were not treated as an adult in this country for many many years. It was hard for white people to realise and to understand that just over the bridge – here we are all sitting in this white lovely, covered area – when, in the townships, there was just chaos. You know, if you grew up in a white suburb, like we did, you'd see black people stepping off the pavement when they approached you, and they never looked into your face.

I think, where I had my first sort of injection of what was going on was the period when many people, young people, died on the streets. It was really devastating. There was one funeral after the other. Those funerals fuelled the fire of activism. That was quite a stage in our life when we could say that a change has to happen. People were no longer accepting the Bantu Education. They were no longer happy with the fact that people were dying.

We heard years later that one of our neighbours was spying on us and he was an informer. He used to work in his garage and watched everything that was going on in our flat.

I could never describe to you the fear that people lived with in those times, because you never knew who was with you and who was against you. You knew that the NP [Nationalist Party, the ruling party during the apartheid era], they paid you to spy on people. They became the 'third force' in that struggle. They turned black against black. Forced people to set fire to their own people's houses and to spy on their own people. If you were poor and your children didn't have food, you would do that, to get paid for it. In fact this incident happened with us as well.

In 1986 Lawrence was detained; he was taken away from our house and put in prison and I was alone at home with the children. That was really, really hard. We heard years later that one of our neighbours was spying on us and he was an informer. He used to work in his garage and watched everything that was going on in our flat. Much later his wife came to ask for forgiveness because of what happened. She realised that it was really bad. Lawrence chose not to forgive her. If it has happened in our small place to one person, imagine what has happened in the country. That made me understand that this is bigger and there is a third force everywhere.

It was on one of those days of the funerals that a young pupil was buried; he had been shot in gunfire. When Lawrence and his class came back from that funeral, a tank – they called it 'Mellow Yellow' – was waiting for them. They were coming out of a side road, crossing over that road where the tank was waiting. They couldn't cross the road except by passing the tank. The people got very angry. It wouldn't have angered the students to see a tank there, but they just buried someone who was shot by one of those people. The guy in the tank said to Lawrence, 'You got one minute to disperse, otherwise we are going to open fire!'. This guy called Lawrence a 'kaffir lover' and bad things like that. Lawrence was so terrified he just turned around and started running, and he ran and ran and ran, and a car stopped for him and took him to our home. He left his students there. He had to run for his life, because they would have shot him. If he hadn't run away, they would have shot him. And he got home and he couldn't speak for an hour. I knew that something terrible had happened. Then he started crying and he described to me what had happened and I got so angry inside. That was the first time that I ever really started saying 'enough is enough'.

Then I joined a women's movement, the ANC Women's League, once they were unbanned. By then I worked in the townships. Tried to learn, what is this all about, why is there a struggle? I developed my own understanding. I had to find out about all of these things. Then I realised that my role in South Africa as a woman is much bigger than just having children and being there for my husband.

Avril Hoepner ::

^ Toddlers having their afternoon nap at a daycare centre in Guguletu.

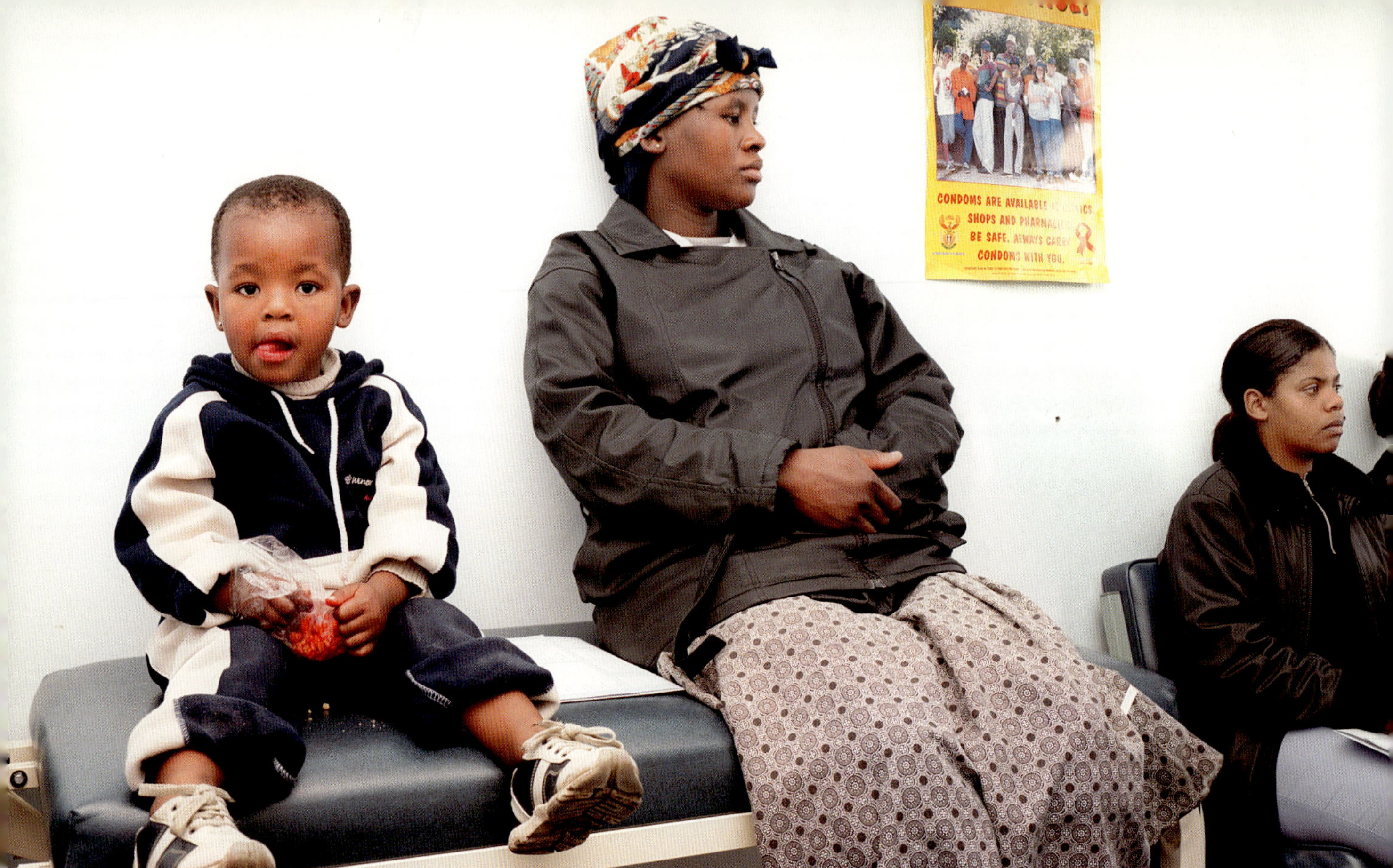

They don't know that the HIV-virus can't be transmitted by shaking hands.

^ Sharon Kelderman teaching Aids prevention to women in a hospital on the Cape Flats. **Sophia Loum** (48) heads up the Sothemba organisation.

Sothemba started in 1992, as a volunteer group, because, in this area [Bellville, north of Cape Town], people with HIV/Aids were not really supported, not at all. The only supporting group was in Cape Town, but there was nothing out here, because this is more an Afrikaans conservative community.

At that time it was a topic that wasn't discussed. It was just something that was very far and it was stigmatised a lot more than today. The perception then was that it is a homosexual disease. It wasn't well known that it is in fact a heterosexual disease as well.

We realised there are people that are HIV-positive and there is no help. This is basically how it started. Some community leaders or role players were coming together, discussing this whole issue. There were people from the welfare, people from the medical field and just ordinary people, for example business people and housewives.

We started doing educational work. We concentrated on training women's groups, youth and school groups. We were incorporating people that live with HIV into our Aids education, which was quite good, because it had a stronger impact on the audience. Then they met someone who would say, 'I'm living with HIV, I'm living with the virus, I'm HIV-positive,' and all of a sudden they could see, oh, this is just an ordinary person, and you could look that person in the eyes, and you realise it just could have been me. That changed people's perception and their attitude a lot.

Why are so many people in southern Africa infected with Aids? There are a lot of different reasons. It has to do with a lack of education. Many people don't really understand how it can be that you can live with the virus, but you are healthy. I mean, this is a contradiction. How can I be HIV-positive but don't feel pain anywhere, or don't have a sore? I can't see it, so how can I be ill? It is not a reality for that person, so why would that person believe that it is transmitted through sexual practice? I might start thinking, 'No man, they just don't want me to have pleasure or they don't want me to produce children.'

This remains from the history where we are coming from. There are a lot of people that are not literate, and the apartheid system enhanced the fact that the educational level of the African people wasn't that high. Even today I see children that don't go to school because their parents can't afford it, which is a pity. How will they discipline children who are not going to school? The parents have to work during the day and the children are on the streets. Many of the children at the moment, and I also foresee that for the future, will be absorbed in other families, when their parents have died of Aids.

We want to encourage people to walk in and to say 'I want to know my HIV status'. I don't know why, but sometimes it is easier just to ignore something than to face it.

And these families also suffer; they struggle with their own children and now they have extra children to care for. We find, even among our educated communities, some ignorance. Maybe it is a kind of deliberate ignorance, like, 'I don't want to know.'

But today there is definitely more understanding about this problem.

Do they get any support from the government, maybe drugs? I think at the moment the government can't afford to hand out the anti-retrovirals to the people [since this interview was conducted, the government initiated free ARV treatment]. I think, if we concentrate more on the treatment of HIV-infected people, we can keep them healthy. We have seen that. None of the people around us are on anti-retroviral medication. They can keep themselves healthy by a good diet. Proper accommodation is important because, in the winter, they live out in places where it is wet and cold, and some of them don't even have a bed to sleep on. They obviously will get ill easier than someone that eats well and stays warm. And also, if the illness is treated soon enough, the person can stay healthy longer. And then they can look after their children themselves and raise their children themselves.

So do you think the anti-retroviral medication is not necessary? The thing with ARV is that it has to be taken at a specific time that you shouldn't miss, because otherwise you create resistance against the drug. It might be wrong to focus on ARV in a community where the people are not educated, because it is difficult to follow the treatment schedule. I think the way to go is to focus on the basic things. ARV treatment will however bring a positive outlook on the epidemic.

Will there be a better future? Yes, there are rewards. You know, you look at people and you remember how they came in here for the first time, betrayed, anxious, afraid, after being diagnosed HIV-positive. In a month you see that the person has relaxed, become more confident about their HIV status. You see that someone could become positive about life again. To look at themselves positively in the end, in terms of, 'Ah, I'm not a bad person and I'm going to manage all the things and I'm going to raise my children.'

We want to encourage people to walk in and to say, 'I want to know my HIV status.' I don't know why, but sometimes it is easier just to ignore something than to face it. They would rather like to believe that they are not HIV-positive. But we want them to face it, to be responsible for that. With the destigmatisation of the illness it will become much better, but at the moment it is still too much stigmatised. If I come out tomorrow and I'm HIV-positive, then maybe my family, the people in my church, my children at school, maybe they don't want to talk about it, you know. It is a pity that it is like that. That we can't just see it as another illness, like cancer. If my mother got cancer, no-one would look down on her. They would rather say, 'Oh, I'm so sorry to hear that.' They don't know the HIV-virus can't be transmitted by shaking hands, for example. We treat HIV-positive people like human beings, like ordinary people and they look after themselves in a better way. That brings a positiveness into themselves. That's what people with HIV need.

Sophia Loum ::

^ Graffiti with a social message in Grahamstown.

<< Goodwood, a middle-class suburb in Cape Town (pages 60–61).

^ Typical middle-class suburban houses in Cape Town.

Apartheid? We learned about that in school.

> BMX riders in Bellville, Cape Town.

What are you doing?

Kyle (16): We are riding our BMXs. We built these little ramps out of mud so that we can can jump with our bikes. But sometimes we get trouble from the police and we have to tear it down again. Then we go to other places and start again. Sometimes we go to BMX contests, where you can win a prize: money, or parts for your bikes.

Have you won anything yet?

Kyle: No, not yet. We just started.

What do you want to do when you finish school?

Kyle: Don't know yet. As a hobby I would like to do motocross. I'd like to go maybe overseas, when I finish school in two years' time. Maybe London or America.

Nicholas (13): I would like to get a good education and good work.

What work do you want to do?

Nicholas: I actually surf. My main thing is surfing. I want to surf at all the good places. Every weekend we go surfing, but the work I want to learn is to be a mechanic.

Daniel (14): I would like to be a computer programmer or something like that.

Do you know anything about apartheid?

Kyle: Apartheid? We learned about that in school.

Do you think it is finished now?

Kyle: Half, half. There are still people going on with that stuff.

Do you have coloured or black friends?

Kyle: Ja, a lot of them. But some of them don't like you.

Nicholas: There are a lot of gangs around. The Rough Riders and the Taxi Boys and stuff like that. And they are dangerous and they deal with drugs.

Did you have problems with them?

Ali (10): Ja, they wanted to rip my bike off.

Do you have any wishes for the future?

Daniel: Ja, that the blacks and the whites live together, without fighting. The crime must come to an end.

Kyle: I wish that I could have work so that I can look after my family and give them some money.

Kyle, Nicholas, Daniel and Ali ::

'6
1610 161016 10 161016
BILLABON

MONT

^ Sunday excursion to Camps Bay, Cape Town.

<< Local football supporters at Hartleyvale in Observatory, Cape Town (pages 66–67).

^ Bowling club in Camps Bay.

< ^ Bowling club in Constantia, Cape Town.

We have divided hearts. I am homesick for Namibia, for South West. Germany would interest me, but I would not like to live there. They drive on the wrong side; do you know why?

Have you ever been to Germany? No, I've never been there. *Why not?* Because I gave all my money away, to poor people. I actually did want to go to Germany after the war, but I first had to work and post office clerks don't get too much money. My mother was half Polish; my father was born in England, because my grandfather was a great socialist. He always had to flee, because he was half communist, and then he came to South Africa and we had to follow him. First he drove transport for the English here during the war, but then he said, 'Let's go up there [Namibia]; the Germans are there.' Then he blindly sailed on a ship to Swakopmund, jumped into the water and reached land. After his arrival, he built a house for his rather large family: there were eight kids.

We were very free under the South African government. Except that, during the war, they imprisoned all the Germans, inluding my father, as they were all supposed to be Hitler's supporters, which we were. But back then Hitler was, how do you say, the man, in Germany. And, when the war came, we wanted to be only German, that is all. Then they interned lots of people. There were prison camps in South Africa; that's where most of the Germans spent the war.

South Africa was at war with Namibia for a very short time. They came in and the Germans had a small defence force and defeating them was child's play. The English ships – the warships came from the coast.

Did you actually experience apartheid? Yes, they brought the apartheid system to Namibia as well. It went like this: in the old days, the German aristocracy would send the black sheep of their families to Africa, you see, and then they would send telegrams back home, saying: 'Send money or we're coming back!' [laughing] Many of them married the blacks, especially the Hereros. And that is a meanness of the German government: they gave the Hereros nothing, but the communists gave them [the Hereros] money. The Hereros were a tribe caught in the middle. They started a revolt, and then the Germans obviously started shooting and the Hereros escaped. The Germans wanted the Hereros as labourers. They escaped out of the ring that the Germans created around them, and they fled into the desert and died, most of them. And that's where Germany could have helped a bit. The Hereros all spoke German and wore traditional

> **Alfred Gürtel** (77) grew up in Namibia and now lives in a German old age home in Cape Town.

<< An old woman walking home, Klein Constantia, Cape Town (pages 72–73).

We were not nasty to them. We said to them: 'Okay, we have apartheid. There is your land. Develop yourselves.'

German clothes. Now, you see, the Afrikaans language is easier than German, but even so, many coloureds learned it [German]. Half-castes, quite white. While we say '*Brot*' and the Afrikaners say '*Brood*', they say, for example '*Broatt*'. So, you see, a very small difference.

Have you never wanted to go to Germany? Yes sure, naturally! I could even have gone for free. I have friends in Germany, they are millionaires who invited me. But you can't accept charity from people. They were here and I helped them with shopping. The old granny was here in the old age home for a few months, but she didn't like it. She always called me 'my Gürtelchen'. I've never seen a snowfall [laughing], never. Once in Johannesburg, it started to snow. Oh, that was cold.

What I wanted to say was, the blacks don't have a written language. Below the equator, no language has developed, not in South America and not in Australia. Maybe the Bushmen, they painted on walls. But there wasn't such a thing as a written language at all. You asked them, 'What is house?' 'Yes, house is called *kaya*.' 'So how do you write *kaya*?' 'We don't have writing.' So the Europeans had to show them writing, exactly how the Arabians taught the Europeans numbers, and that's how the blacks then learned to write their language. We were not nasty to them. We said to them, 'Okay, we have apartheid. There is your land. Develop yourselves.' We put millions into it, no billions. The one built a whole airport. No plane ever comes there. The homelands were really beautiful; that was green country. Every year in Lesotho, every year in winter, we have to send blankets and things. They never think ahead. Whenever it gets cold, they freeze. Oh well, what can you do then? We are labelled as Nazis. Look here, the Germans and the Belgians are white. A Belgian and a German are white, but they have two states. The one is Catholic perhaps and the other Evangelical and that is the biggest difference. Here the cultures of the blacks are totally different from each other. In Europe the culture is the same, and so on. We have different languages, we have hygiene, all those things. The differences are just so much bigger.

In District Six they threw out the coloureds. There was urine running in the streets and the children were half-naked, terrible. The houses all belonged to the foreigners. There was a house, a sister once told me – she taught midwifery there – the people who lived there came in the evening and slept until midnight. At midnight they had to get out. Then the others came and they slept from midnight until seven o'clock in the morning. That's how they exploited them. Then the government built a railway line down to Mitchell's Plain, and built rows and rows and rows and rows of houses there, and built new areas for them. I mean, it was very unfair. 'Yes,' they said, 'these old dwellings are full of rats and the slums must be demolished.' They said that something new would be built one day. But, you know, those areas are still open with no buildings.

What comes to mind, when you think about Germany? We were obviously all shocked when Schröder came to power, not so? I mean, it is good if there is a change and the new government tries to put right the wrongs of the previous one. The whole of Europe will wake up one day if the Islamic extremists cause more terror for them. I mean, it can't carry on like that.

Do you think of yourself as an African or a German? Divided in my heart. We have divided hearts. I am homesick for Namibia, for South West. Germany would interest me, but I would not like to live there. They drive on the wrong side; do you know why? Quite simple: it has to do with riding horses. When you sit on a horse and face your enemy, you need to make sure that you pass them on the side furthest from your heart, the left-hand side. That way you protect your heart and it is exactly the same when you're driving. I'm all for driving on the left-hand side. It is much better in case of an accident. Just think about it: horses are the same as cars. I have no idea why one should drive on the right. Because, if you drive on the right, then your heart is right there on the side of the traffic.

Alfred Gürtel ::

^ A traffic light knocked over by someone driving on the wrong side of the road, Killarney, Cape Town.

2002-12-31

> **Greenthumb** (22) (on the left), a DJ, with a friend in Rosebank, Johannesburg.

<< On a street in Prince Albert, Karoo (pages 78–79).

I used to be part of a gang, but not, like, very deeply involved. Luckily hip-hop came at the right time and pulled me out.

< **Ready D** (33), DJ and producer of *Universal Souljaz*, one of South Africa's first hip-hop bands.

I was born and raised in District Six until we were forced to move and thrown into the Cape Flats in an area known as Mitchell's Plain. Mitchell's Plain is on a basic level. A couple of hundred thousands of years ago the area was covered by the sea. When the Dutch came here they kind of colonised the Cape. They were looking for places to build prisons and Mitchell's Plain was one of the areas that they suggested, but then they found out that it was an area that wasn't suitable for human conditions, because it was impossible to build on the soil.

Mitchell's Plain is heavily gun infested. It's probably the area on the Cape Flats that has the most gangs. One gang could easily have a membership of up to 110 000 members spreading all over the Cape Flats, including other cities in other countries as well. Though we're looking at gangs like the Americans, the Hard-Livings, the Fancy Boys, the Euro Cats, the Sexy Boys, the Firm Boys, the School Boys, the Dixies, the Cool Cats, the Beach Cats, the Funky Americans, the Ugly Americans and the list goes on and on. A lot of the gangs were used in the days of apartheid as a form of informer for the previous government, and in exchange they were allowed to push their drugs and also get weapons from the army and government.

So which means a lot of the kids on the Cape Flats have little alternative, you know. Because of the situation: the education system – its shortage of schools, teachers, the type of education that people are given. But besides all the problems it's a lot of fun people, a lot of lovely people and a lot of educated people on the Cape Flats as well.

The gangs fight against each other and they also fight amongst people in the community. There are a lot of kids that are dying in the crossfire. Schools are closed on a regular basis because of gang warfare. They use school grounds as battlefields. The major reason why people are fighting is the control of territory. If you control the area it means you can push the drugs and the guns. Part of the war, besides territory, is also a young and a new generation of gangsters coming up right now. It's a very young generation, that ranges between the age of five till about in his late teens and that's a hard-living gangster. He's not afraid of nobody and he's not afraid to die and not afraid to kill, to murder. A lot of the older

All that I need is a bit of land where I can grow my fruit, my veg, so I can eat and have a roof over my head.

gangs are afraid of these kids coming up because in the old gang system there used to be laws and principals. A lot of the young kids had killed a lot of the top gang leaders. It's completely out of control and the reason for that is obviously because of the previous apartheid system. I blame it on that government and I blame it on the government today as well. Economics, education, school systems, hospital systems, the integration facility has been divided up according to skin colour, texture of their hair, size of their lips. I mean the area where I'm staying is dominated by Muslim people. They were put here for a purpose. Just across the road you find more darker skinned people. They were put there for specific reasons. Then you cross the train line and you get people that are classified and qualified as so-called Africans or blacks. If you trace our roots, all go to common ancestors. In the previous government they divided the people. The true country has been destroyed, a lot of the languages have died out and there is only a handful of the true original people.

People were situated and split. A lot of District Six people were all split up. The people came from all different areas and were thrown into Mitchell's Plain as neighbours. So the one person found out, 'Damn, that's my enemy living next door, he's from another gang', and that one found out, 'Oh shit, there's another gang living there'. That's also what contributed to the violence.

District Six was a very musical community. I'd say it was musically driven. My father, my family, my ancestors, that's definitely where it all started for me. But recently I have always been the one to play the music. Even for the older crowd as a little kid, five to six years old, I was always there with a big eight-track recorder pushing in the cassettes, playing the records for the older kids. That's kinda where it started and from then it has been probably a natural attraction to me.

When I heard the first hip-hop song I could immediately relate to what the MC was saying. Some of the music that we manage to get was through a lot of our friends. The older guys, they used to work on the ships and they used to travel overseas.

I grew up with all those things like reggae, funk, soul, jazz, blues, hip-hop, Cape traditional music. The only thing I didn't grow up with was more sort of African tribal traditional music because we were made to believe that it isn't our kind of music; they call it 'music for kaffirs'. Later we started doing research and started realising, you know, all the bullshit that was put in your head when you were a little kid. The time when hip-hop started taking the black consciousness course was when South Africa reached its peak in the riots. In 1987 state of emergency and all that stuff was coming up. That is probably the period when we became more conscious and became more pro-African and Pan-African.

I used to have a lot of friends that were serious gang members. I mean, I used to be part of a gang, but not, like, very deeply involved. Luckily hip-hop came at the right time and it pulled me out of that sort of situation.

I would say we [Prophets of da City] were the first hip-hop crew to record and establish ourselves in the music market. On the second album one song was officially banned and one of the videos was edited, because we had a photo of the previous president, PW Botha. We put his picture in a fridge and told him to chill out. That wasn't suitable with the SABC, which was government controlled. They banned the video and it had to be edited. The ironic part is that SABC shot the video. That's how messed up they were.

It's a law of nature. You go through a period and then you have to experience tumult. After the tumult will come the calm and the peace, because then people will be more enlightened and aware of the spirits. You try everything to make life easier, it's all gonna turn around and backfire on you. Then you gonna go, 'Oh shit, all that I need is a bit of land where I can grow my fruit, my veg, so I can eat, and I need a roof over my head. This is what it is all about.' I need to make a connection to my creator and I gotta be cool with you and you be cool with me and that's what it's all about. Just on a basic and fundamental level. At the end of the day, just on a basic level, we can be cool with one another. I can learn from you, you can learn from me. We can get get along, we can move.

Ready D ::

^ Inside Ready D's home-recording studio.

> **Clifton** (51), a typical Cape character.

^ District Six is an area near Cape Town's city centre. Coloured and black inhabitants were forcibly moved out of here from 1968 to the early '80s.

At least we had bread on our table when the white man ruled. Now that Africans rule, there is fuck all on our table. We have to struggle.

< **Henry** (43) grew up in District Six. Today he lives on the Cape Flats as a result of the forced removals.

I'm staying here for 20 years now. I was born in District Six and I grew up there. But we were forced to move out to other places like Mitchell's Plain, Manenberg and Hanover Park. They split us up and they took us away from each other. That is what they used to do. But things have changed now. We try to make Cape Town better than it was before.

Mandela promised people things, like a new fridge. He promised people a stove, but he never gave a person even one thing. But he promised, 'People come to my side. I give you a stove. Come to my side, vote for me for your new president.' I was there on the Parade when he made his promises to a lot of people.

What do you think about the new president? The new president? Ha, you are talking about someone who knows nothing. He can't even rule this world. I can tell you one thing about South Africans: all they can do is scratch in the dirt bins, and that is the honest truth. Listen, because if you rule the world, I mean, if your country is ruling the world, how can it be that the people scratch in other people's dirt bins? That is not ruling of South Africans. South Africans stand up for their rights! I mean like I do. I rather work for my bread. I won't go scratching in dirt bins looking for food or old clothes. I mean, what is the good of that?

Do you remember the time when the bulldozers came? That was 1978, yeah, I remember the time. I was little, but I can tell you they had no mercy for our people. Even the white people had no mercy. But at least we had bread on our table when the white man ruled this world. But now that the Africans rule this world, there is fuck all on our table. We have to struggle. We have to struggle.

So that means the Africans can't rule this world, because they are still going to the white man, asking for information, how to do this and how to do that. They can't do anything on their own. All they can do is promise, promise and they do nothing. They don't care about the coloureds. That is why we stand up for our own rights, not for African rights, not for the white men's rights.

I came here every day. Every day I came here, because this is my country. I lived in this country, I mean District Six. I was born in District Six and I hope I'm going to die in District Six. But I know I'm not going to die here, because I live in Mitchell's Plain, me and my wife. Here I'm at home, because I walked up here barefoot, like him [pointing at a little boy].

'Piesang', my mother said, 'come and get your food.' They called me Piesang – that is my nickname. My nickname is Piesang [banana]. 'Come and fetch your banana' and I ran over to the shop and I got my banana. That is the way we worked and we lived in District Six.

People are making us rather look like animals than human beings, because they gave nothing to us. That's why I'm in trouble. I'm talking about it, because I got too much stress, because what must I do, where am I going to get my money? I learned to beg for money. Not on the streets. I'm not gonna stand on the streets like he does and beg for money. I would rather work like a squirrel looking for food, hiding his food for the winter, trying to survive. I would rather do that, but I would never go on my knees and beg a white man for money or beg a black man for money. He can rather take his money...

I still want to know why they destroyed the people here. Why did they destroy this, because there is nothing here today? It's more than twenty, more than twenty-five years ago now. I'm forty-three years already. I was a young boy, but they did nothing here. Do you know what it is? It's a part of apartheid here in South Africa, you see. So the white man came and pushed all the houses down, to build a technikon. I can't say it's wrong, we need the technikon in Cape Town, but why did they have to move all the people, to build one place? Only to build one place. Taking all of us out and now it's an open land here. That is still a part of apartheid.
Henry ::

^ **Paul Mogamat** (23) outside his shack in District Six.

I got 16 years and six months. Apartheid was very hard in prison. There were organisations: the 26s, the 27s and the 28s. You had to choose one of these organisation.

> **Anthony Booysen** (41) cleans dustbins at the Holiday Inn. He receives cardboard boxes as payment, which he sells to recycling centres.

I was born in District Six the 8th of the 9th month. I grew up here. It was apartheid then. Life was hard. We had to do something to survive. School is a place where you learn something, but you will never learn something good. There the crime is starting. I went to prison for armed robbery, it was 1982. So I went to prison and I got sixteen years and six months. Apartheid was very hard in prison. There were organisations: the 26s, the 27s and the 28s. You had to choose your own organisation. The 27s, they are the people who believe in blood. The 26s believe in *kroon* or money, and the 28s use sodomy. So I joined the organisation of the 26s, because we were fighting for rights – civil rights, human rights and stuff like that. They didn't give these rights to us, the white man. If you wanted to be a member of one of the three organisations, you had to draw blood, you had to show them that you fight the white man. If you didn't fight the white man, the organisation didn't accept you.

The organisations started in the mines. The white people killed the black in the mines. If you died in the mines, they didn't let your parents know. It came out of the mines into the prisons and today it is still in the prisons. The war is still on in the prisons. These organisations, they were like the ANC [African National Congress] or the PAC [Pan-Africanist Congress] in prison. We fought for our rights, like our president [Mandela], who was also in prison. He fought from the inside to the outside. We didn't fight the way he fought. We had to draw blood. If you stab the warden, they don't take you to the court for your crime. First they do their own thing, after that they take you to court. There are gangsters in the prison and gangsters outside the prison and the government is in the middle and they don't know what to do. They haven't got no solution for it. Ask me, I'm out of it. Do you see my head here? That's the way I got hurt by the wardens in prison, with big sticks. That time they didn't talk, they just hit you. I got too many bumps on my head from prison. Not from outside, from inside the prison, behind closed doors.

I've been there for sixteen years and six months. I lost my mother and I lost my father. That's why I'm living like that, but I try to make an honest living. I don't want to go back there. It is no life there, the only life there is hard. You see, this time of the day, I couldn't sit with you. I'm locked up,

The main thing is, they must try to stop gangsterism. That's all I want. Then this is going to be the sweetest country in the whole world.

till tomorrow morning. They open your door at eight o'clock in the morning, for breakfast. Exercise is only one hour. At eleven o'clock you get your supper. After that you get no food till tomorrow morning. That time we slept on the floor. Two mats and three blankets, no matter if it was summer or winter. We had to sleep on the floor. There were forty people in one room. You had no privacy, you got nothing. Some of them got robbed. When you had soap or toilet stuff, they robbed you. If we wanted to watch TV, we had to pay thirty rand for the TV for the weekend. You had to sell your bread, tobacco and your soup to get the money. But I don't know where the money goes. Nobody knows where the money goes. But it's us who want to see soccer, want to see rugby, want to to see cricket, and the main thing was the news. We want to see the news, want to see what they were doing in the outside world. That's why there is so much violence in prison. Violence will never stop in prison. Blood will never end in prison. I saw a man eating another man's heart. I saw it with my eyes. He cut him open and ate his heart. They hung him for that. Nowadays there is no real change in prison. Apartheid is alive in all South African prisons. It's the white man who made us the way we are today. It goes from generation to generation to generation. It will never end. It is in our veins. They put it in our veins.

I came out on the third of January that year. I know that it was a long time. I can't do it in three months, but I try. I'm scared of the town, the way the life is today. I'm scared to go outside, because I don't want to be involved in crime again. I clean bins there by the Holiday Inn and I get some cardboard boxes and I go and sell them. It's for a living for my family. They don't pay me, because of the tattoos I got in prison. I can't get a permanent job because of this.

What was it like when you came out into democracy? I was glad. Not for me actually, but for the generation. Here is a life for them now. Before that time, it was hard. In 1976, it was a big riot here. On 16th of June, a lot of people died, a lot of children died. 16th of June 1976. You must never forget that. There was a song out, 'Teachers leave them kids alone. We don't need no education'. It was for the children who were fighting for civil rights. That's why they sing the song.

The children from now, they are broad-minded, my friend, they are born broad-minded. You see the games they play, the computer games. Sometimes I go to a shop here and I stay there for half an hour to see the children, how they play the computer games. Then my mind says, 'Where was I when this thing was?' I didn't have that privilege. I see computers, but if you ask me how to work with computers or what to do on a computer, I don't know. I only see that this is a computer, but I don't know how to work with it.

The other day I went for my ID [to apply for his identity document]. She asked me when I was born. I told her when I was born and where I was born. She pressed buttons there and I saw everything that I've done in my life. She showed it to me there on the screen. I was shocked. I was shocked. I asked that lady, 'Lady, how do you know about that?' and she told me, 'This is in the computer.' And I also told her a small piece of my life.

Now there is the chance for the children to carry on. I hope the children now accept it. Because the schools are together; there is no more coloured one side, white one side. They are together. The languages are all together. English, Xhosa, Afrikaans. But those children who are dead, who were fighting, they sacrificed their life for this.

It's the same in prison. A lot of my friends, they sacrificed themselves, for the rights in prison. There are some rights now. You can go to your mother's funeral. If your mother is in hospital, you can go and visit her. That is the result of the sacrificing. But the main thing is they must try to stop gangsterism. That's all I want. Then this is going to be the sweetest country in the world.

Anthony Booysen ::

^ Anthony's sister with her son, holding a toy gun.

Star
MART
WOOLWORTHS

< Anti-firearm demonstration in Cape Town's city centre.

>> Viglietti Motors, Gardens, Cape Town, sells luxury cars (page 102); **Mishka Veldman**, who works in the plastic surgery industry, Camps Bay (page 103).

We don't want to kill the golden goose or destabilise the economy. We need the economy to grow and we want people to start sharing in the economy.

> **Letepe Maisela** (45) is Managing Director and founder of two companies in Johannesburg.

In the '70s I went to the University of the North, one of the tribal universities, to study Social Sciences. When I completed that, I went to work in Soweto. I was there when Soweto '76 exploded. I was very young, in my early 20s. I stayed there until 1990. When the old man left the island [Mandela left Robben Island], I also left Soweto.

In Soweto I worked for a community centre, dealing with the youth. When '76 exploded, I was actually one of the youth leaders. We were not members of the ANC. You must remember the ANC was banned. We were supporters. We protested. We got arrested very often at that time. The people don't understand that the type of activism we went through was not an activism of toting machine guns and firing in the air. It was a form of resistance and it was not the passive resistance of Martin Luther King or Mahatma Gandhi. It was something above that. It was conscious resistance. It was not just passive; we were very active. But we stopped short of violence.

In the '80s I had a marketing promotions company with a friend of mine in Jo'burg. We couldn't register the company in our name. We had to get a white nominee although it was our company. In terms of the Johannesburg by-laws of the time, black people were not allowed to hold keys to an office. So you were not allowed to open an office after hours or to lock it at night. So we had to let the white guy come in the morning, open for us, go away, come in the afternoon, close for us and go away.

Today, where we are, we have just started another struggle. The first one was political, now we are in the second phase, which is economic. We in South Africa were the first on the continent to coin the expression 'black economic empowerment'. Many countries in Africa were independent before us and they didn't have that. To them life went on as usual. In Zimbabwe they did nothing until two years ago, when old Bob [Robert Mugabe] woke up and started talking about economic empowerment of his own people. They never did that before, but we taught them that. We learned from their mistake that having political power is not sufficient if the economy is still in the control of the colonisers. The colonialists, all they did was to relinquish political power and retain economic power. We said, 'No, that is not fair.' The economic power was based on the resources of this country, so there should be an element of sharing. We didn't say they must give it up; we said they must share. We are not looking at taking over the economic power, but it is a process and the process started in 1994. Now in 2004, ten years later, we are still grappling with the issues of economical empowerment. But we are getting somewhere, because, as you can see, there have been a lot of charters recently: the Mining Charter, the Oil Industry Charter. All the charters have got one thing in common: they want to ensure that the slices of the cake are shared equitably among all South African peoples. One cannot ignore the factor of race, because it is still a fact that those people who have the mince are white people, and those who haven't got the mince are black people. Those people who employ are white people and the employees are black people. We don't want to kill the golden goose or destabilise the economy. We need the economy to grow and we want people to start sharing in the economy. So it is a very tough act, for government, for the corporate world, for us.

Not much has changed for people of my calibre since 1994. For the man in the street – who before 1994 did not have running water, did not have an electric bulb in his house, did not have a telephone line – it has changed. On my level, what has changed is that I now own shares in companies. I play the stock market. So that has changed. The only thing is that the change at my level has been limited to too few people. There is only a small clique of people up there who are the shining light, and everybody seems to be focusing on them. What we're trying to say is the change needs to be spread; it must cascade downwards to the broad masses of this country. For instance, it does not help to have running water, electricity, a telephone, if you are unemployed. Make sure that people have employment. The talk today is: do something that is sustainable. There has been change. It is a process, and maybe ten years is not enough time.

I am what I am today in spite of apartheid, not because of it. I don't moan about those years, because it is over. I'm not going to waste my energy crying over spilled milk. What we need to do now is to make this country work. Let's make sure that the economic cake is shared equally by all of us.
Letepe Maisela ::

CLICK

< A street scene in Johannesburg's central business district.

SPORTS
CHAMPIONS

The Bo-Kaap is a Muslim region on the slopes of Lion's Head, adjacent to Cape Town's city centre:

^ Boys playing on the street.

> **Gamien Najaar** (51) is the muezzin [caller] of the Nur-ul Houda Mosque.

<< After a game of street football, Cape Town (pages 108–109).

The idea was to find a way to reintroduce our history to people so that it is part of popular culture, through celebrating people who brought us here, like Steve Biko.

> **Nkhensani Manganyi** (30) is the founder of the Stoned Cherrie fashion label based in Johannesburg.

The bulk of my life that I remember was spent in Johannesburg, but I grew up in place called Diepkloof in Soweto. I have memories of a happy childhood, but it was a very strange time. I was very aware of what was going on in the country then. My strongest memory of that time was when I was about sixteen and my sister was beaten up by some AWB [Afrikaner Weerstandsbeweging, a right-wing organisation] guys. We had gone on a picnic to Santorama and they beat her up badly. It was a man and his family, they had been drinking and started threatening the people. As my sister came back to tell me not to come, they hit her on the head with a bottle and kicked her in the face. We were with one guy, but the rest of us were girls. Later on, while we were waiting to be fetched, one of their little boys came and the guy who was with us wanted revenge; he wanted to hit him with a brick. We all said, 'No,' because he was just a child. For me it was such a defining moment, because I thought: that is the difference between them and us.

I studied Industrial Psychology and Sociology at Wits [University of the Witwatersrand in Johannesburg]. After I'd finished my degree, I didn't really want to do psychology at the time, so I got into theatre. I did a number of productions and I travelled. As I travelled I was very inspired by the African aesthetic that exists on the continent, that can't be replicated anywhere else in the world. It's African. I was intrigued by the thought that we hadn't created a brand that was an expression of this urban energy and this life.

In 2000 I started Stoned Cherrie, a brand that is basically a celebration of South African icons. 'Cherry' in township lingo means 'woman': 'my cherry' is 'my woman'. The inspiration for it was to try and create something that would celebrate these women, these strong, amazing women that have come out of our soils. Not famous women that everybody knows. Just women in the streets that sacrificed, that have had to live in rural areas as their husbands go and work on mines. And they have to bring up families and sometimes the husbands disappear. There is an inherent strength that makes them continue to be mothers, continue to teach and love. So basically I was inspired to create a brand that would be an expression of what I refer to as Afro-urban culture, because all representations of Africa have been through eyes of people who haven't necessarily lived here and they haven't allowed those stories to tell themselves. For instance, you always see a glorification of certain tribes or a leopard print: the safari experience is always the interpretation of Africa. It is just a foreign arms-length interpretation.

Stemming from my interest in psychology, I think that, even though we have undergone the changes we have been through, there is still a lot of reparation that needs to take place. Psychologically you can't go through an era of repression and not have psychological ramifications.

So I always have been passionate that there needs to be a healing process, whether it is through psychologists, or through institutions, or through education, theatre, film or fashion. Part of my vision was then to speak to young South Africans in a way that is palatable to them and is exciting: 'Don't talk to me about politics,' you know. One of the things that we did was approach Bailey's African History Archives [created by Jim Bailey, founder of *Drum* magazine]. For me it was interesting, because it was the first real documentation of the '50s urban culture. It was a very interesting era of self-expression and it has always intrigued me that during that time, when there was a lot of political repression, people were vibrant and dancing and there were supermodels. So people lived, people made a way to live. Basically the idea was to find a way to reintroduce our history to people so that it is part of popular culture, through celebrating people who brought us here, like Steve Biko. But doing it in a way that speaks to young people. That perhaps at some point will inspire them to go and read up more and use the archive, because there they can find out more about these people and what they did and what their significance was.

We came at an interesting time, because a lot of South Africans, black and white, were looking for an identity. Our customers are very mixed. It is not just the black market: we have a very big white market and a big foreign market. It appeals more to a head-space than a demographic. For us it's about instilling a sense of pride and identity in a unified way, because I think that putting too much emphasis on the differences in culture separates people. I think we need to start seeing beyond those things that divide us.
Nkhensani Manganyi ::

My ideal is that a woman doesn't see herself in terms of colour. She just sees herself as a combination of emotions, interests, passions and concerns. It sounds naïve but this is just entertainment.

> **Vanessa Raphaely** (38) is the Editorial Director of Associated Magazines.

My mother started this company [Jane Raphaely and Associates, now called Associated Magazines] almost twenty-one years ago and I was in London at that point.

Cosmopolitan is twenty years old now. It started right in the middle of apartheid. Compared to the *Cosmos* in other countries there is quite a dramatic difference. The South African *Cosmo* is positioned more upmarket; it's somewhat older, and it's more concerned with affirmation, empowerment and encouragement of young women. The British *Cosmo* for example is very much concerned with the search for sex and so is the American. It's a very small little universe. Because of what it's like to be a young woman in South Africa, it's much more about making them feel happy with the choices they've made. Making them feel empowered to live in a country that's actually quite challenging. If you are a young independent woman in South Africa, it throws some really serious challenges at you. The way we do it here is we go for the stuff that unites women, not that divides us. Every woman in her twenties, no matter what race, we believe is concerned about the search for love, the desire to succeed at work and a certain degree of material pleasure. This is not for all women, it's for an already emerged black woman, as much as it is for an affirmed, empowered white woman. It's basically been about really finding a spirit that a large percentage of women in this country identify with, and just working that. Being absolutely sure of what the brand is, being proud of it as well. Over the last year and a half we have grown by sixteen percent, and it was the market leader even at sixteen percent less. I don't think there is anything like that in the world; certainly no *Cosmos* in the world have had that kind of performance. *Cosmo* has 40:60 percent in white to black, coloured and Indian, which is the best you can expect, at R21.95. It's expensive for a local magazine.

Cosmo is perceived as a very colour-blind magazine in this country. We have always had black women writing in it, black women pictured in it. Even all the way back to 1984 we had the first black woman on a cover, but I'm not sure.

When I started working in the UK on women's magazines, I was told categorically, 'You can't put a black woman on a cover of an English magazine.' And you certainly couldn't do that in South Africa; you would take a hit. In *Cosmo* we don't really notice whether she's black or white. We have noticed that as our black content has increased, which is natural, it's been very unconscious, it's just reflecting the changes in the country and the change in our market.

If you page through the magazine, the first three pages are women of colour and, when you go into the magazine, it's neither black nor white; it's just *Cosmo* girls: young attractive women. It's not the colour that motivates us; it has always been the spirit. My ideal is that a woman doesn't see herself in terms of colour. She just sees herself as the combination of emotions, interests, passions and concerns that makes her up. It sounds naïve but this is just entertainment. We are not out there to explain white women and black women to each other. We're explaining why you feel depressed at some point or why you feel frustrated at work or why you keep on fighting with your boyfriend. I don't have a political mission at all.

I came back to South Africa in 1997, and would never have come back if it hadn't become a democracy. So it was only when Madiba was freed and when there were elections. When I came back, there was a euphoria in the beginning which the whole country felt. We were completely high. The white people certainly were high on the fact that we thought we'd got off scot-free. There was a collective sense of, 'Well, that wasn't as bad as we feared it would be.' Of course it takes a long time for the chickens to come back to roost. From a white perspective, there was a kind of relief and a kind of basking: it's like you were the most unpopular girl in the school, and then suddenly you were okay, you got invited to the party. Particularly for my generation, we didn't make apartheid and we benefited from it. But then we rejected it. And now we've come back, and we're still benefiting in some ways, but we're also being punished in some ways. So we're very much a bridging generation. We're neither of one part nor the other. But if you're here you should put something back.

This country is so much better run under the present government than it was, even if you strip away the ethics. In terms of our economic policy we're doing damn great. I think it would be great for kids not to be told in principle by white liberals, but to be shown: people are people.

Vanessa Raphaely ::

AGAZINE IN
FOX

^ **Oliver Gast** (28), a fashion photographer from Germany, at a shoot for an Austrian magazine, Camps Bay, Cape Town.

>> **Dean van Niekerk** (21) and **Simon Kemp** (29), Llandudno, Cape Town (pages 118 and 119).

>>> Llandudno beach (pages 120–121).

AFSEW

The square project attempts to bring into the city a spirit of humaneness. There are those who complain about that, because we have to demolish heritage.

The June 16th uprisings were quite significant. What happened was it was June holidays, so we were fetched from school to come to Ga-Rankuwa. My father thought that the riots, the uprisings, were only in our home village in Ga-Rankuwa. He said to the driver who fetched us: 'Take the children to their cousins in Soweto. You can bring them back when things are more calm.' But Soweto was mad, the madness was at its peak. At the time the government had censored the media from talking about how chaotic the country was. They didn't have a clear picture about where it was worst. So we get to Soweto and it is just a mess and it's at night. We were driving in my father's white Jaguar, so immediately we attracted attention. Anything that had to do with wealth had to be stoned or whatever. We were lucky because my sister was Miss Black South Africa at the time. When these guys came to the car and they were rocking it, she got out and they said, 'No, no, no, it's Rosette Motsepe, Miss South Africa.' So we went through to my aunt's place and there were bullet holes in the ceiling, because they fired at the crowds from the helicopter. We turned around that very night and went to Mmakau [a village in Limpopo Province].

Let's start with the whole idea of how I got to choose to become an architect. It was a mixture of accident and luck or chance. Before I went to university I was applying to study for Law or Economics. At the time, blacks, we weren't becoming architects or specialised in other professions. Your profession was primarily social orientated and either you were a teacher or a lawyer or a doctor. My sister, who was at Harvard at the time, came back from Harvard and said: 'Fanuel, I think you'll like to do Architecture.' The whole family was aware that from childhood onward I was very much into design and into making space. I always wanted to say how the furniture must sit and how to expand the house. When my parents wanted to design the house – this is when I was still a child – I said, 'I'll design it' and I was drawing. I always built shacks, these extraordinary shacks, double-storey shacks, and one had basements. I was very much into building and construction. When I started learning Architecture I knew it was the perfect career choice for me. It flowed with my interests and passions so that first year I just studied like a bulldog. In second year I started to lose interest. It dawned

> **Fanuel Motsepe** (36), a Johannesburg-based architect, is from a Tswana royal family. In order to create a big square that will reflect African heritage, the firm of architect where he works have proposed the demolition of two blocks of buildings in Johannesburg.

<< Johannesburg city centre (pages 122–123).

ADIDAS

Ubuntu attempts to address conflict and misunderstandings. Most important is the relationship between the living and the dead, and God's overall ownership of this system.

on me that all I was learning was about America and Europe. All the bloody time. I thought, 'Where does my home village fit in? Where do we as people fit in? Can I apply these theories and practices at home? Are they suitable?' I went to my head of department and I said to him, 'When are we going to learn about South African architects, what they do? And I don't care if they are black or white.' He said to me 'Forget it, not in this country. If you want to learn about broader approaches to place-making, this is not the country. Here you are only going to get it from the white person's perspective.'

Shortly after UCT [the University of Cape Town] I went to Belgium. Now here is Fanuel Motsepe who has been going on about, 'You are teaching me whites-only nonsense,' and then I go to Belgium, and you can't get more white anywhere else on earth.

I'm very focused on the notion and the realisation that our environment, in terms of humane urban traditions or living traditions, is full of inhumane ways of living traditions. *Ubuntu* is very simply defined by one sentence by which we are all raised: 'You are, because of others.' It's that simple. It does not get more complex than that. It is about the individual being part of a collective and how that collective has interests on the individual, to develop both the individual and the collective. The whole concept of *ubuntu* is about humanity being one big family, and that family is encouraged to live with love, with compassion, with understanding, with tolerance, with patience, with support, with togetherness, with brotherhood, with sisterhood. *Ubuntu* attempts to address conflict and misunderstandings. Most important is the relationship between the living and the dead, and God's overall ownership of this system. So in this concept of *ubuntu* the link to our ancestors is a strong embodiment of how we relate to each other. This concept comes from multiple groups of tribes. All the tribes in southern Africa and in most of Bantu Africa have this concept of *ubuntu* – I've traced it as far up as Nigeria.

The square project attempts to address all that I have said, to bring into the city a spirit of humaneness. There are those who complain about that, because we will have to demolish heritage. We must be very careful when we talk about heritage in South Africa. Who defines heritage? Whose definition of heritage are we forced to adhere to? We must interrogate what is heritage, so that it does embody the diverse views. Because you won't find one definition of what we are. I'm of the opinion that in life, in order to move forward, sacrifices have to be made. To scream and rant and rave because a building is over sixty years old is a problem. Why? Because what makes a building that is two years old culturally insignificant? What? I need someone to explain to me. There are many one-year-old buildings, one of them is the Apartheid Museum or the Hector Petersen memorial. Even a more recent building – Mandela's houses where he is staying now. There is no way that they ever will be demolished. Why not? Because they are culturally significant. Mandela lived there. To take a building that's sixty years old and to bless it with sacred spirit and all that, and then one that is two years old just to spit on it, says to me that somewhere along the line there's a big unanswered question: why is the sixty-year-old one better than the five-year-old one? Why? The argument sometimes is that, because the sixty-year-old one has had three generations, so it has become part of their memory or identity of the place, and I respect that.

Then I'm gonna ask myself, 'Okay, so they are stones in the wall. Now look at what the project proposes: is that not a bigger stone in the wall than the one that you are so concerned about?' Now people say, 'How dare you, you think you put in something more important?'

I think Jo'burg needs places where all cultures are reflected. African identity is not just an indigenous culture, not in today's world. You have now white, Indian, Chinese people in Africa, and they are all Africans because they were born here and they have lived here.

Socially the old Jo'burg died and we just have to go through the city to see how it's dilapidated, to reflect the death of it. There are new lives, new flowers coming out, that give a new identity of Jo'burg. I will never accept the idea of bringing back the old Jo'burg. That means that you must bring back the old prejudices. Jo'burg has to transform. It's that simple.

Fanuel Motsepe ::

^ Fanuel outside one of the houses that he has designed.

36

STOP

32a

Killarney
House
31

^ Gates leading to private residences in Sandton, north of Johannesburg.

If I cut my hair today, by the end of the year I'll be making at least three times more money than I make with dreadlocks.

> **Motamane Mathosi** (29) founder of Mathosi Engineering Services (Pty) Ltd, Johannesburg.

I'm from a place called Polokwane, a small city in Limpopo Province. I'm a mixture of Pedi and Shangane. The name of my tribe is Shangane. My family came from a very poor background; we had cattle and sheep. I did my schooling in Polokwane. I started school in 1981 and I finished matric in 1992. From there I came to Jo'burg, to study Electrical Engineering. I graduated in 1995 at Wits Technikon.

I struggled to get a job because of my dreadlocks. I went to about twenty interviews that lasted at most ten minutes. I had a very strange interview one time. I got into the interview room, the guys were sitting around there, and they said, 'No, we are looking for Mr Mathosi.' I said, 'I am Mr Mathosi.' They started laughing, 'But you look different.' I said, 'I look different from what? You don't have my photo.' I looked different from my results, because I got distinctions throughout my exams. So automatically it was assumed that I can't be that clever and have dreadlocks at the same time. After the interview they would say 'Don't call us, we'll call you.' And you knew that you're not gonna get the job.

And it was like that all the time until I decided to confront people in interviews. So I asked the guys, before we started the interview, 'Listen, guys, before I waste your time, before you waste my time, have you got a problem with my hairstyle?' They looked at each other, and they said, 'No, we don't have a problem with your hairstyle.' And from then on I knew the job was mine, because I broke the barrier, which I'd never managed to do before.

I got the job in 1996 as a graduate electrical engineer. I realised that once I started working my dreadlocks were still a problem, because some of the people working there assumed that I was smoking marijuana and that I was lazy. I worked there [Rand Water] for four years and after that some other guys approached me to become their business partner, in an electrical contracting firm. I joined them for two years. I was a shareholder and a director of the company, which was a big change from Rand Water. I had about sixty people working for me. It was quite tough, I was still very young then. I learned a lot. It is still a problem, with dreadlocks, in the working industry. Especially your accountants, people who wear suits every day. They think it is not a neat look. I constantly had to prove myself to my boss, that I'm good. So that's why I decided to open up my own company, so that I proved to myself that I'm good. And how I proved to myself that I'm good is that my company is still operating, I still have clients. They admit that for most of them it is the first time that they do business with a guy with dreadlocks and they are surprised how clever you are. Sometimes I look at it as irony, because I think, okay, they are surprised at how clever I am, because they didn't expect me to be clever. So, even though I may not be that clever, they think I'm very clever, because they didn't expect anything.

I have got about fifteen engineers working for me now. The name of the company is Mathosi Engineering Services, Mathosi being my surname. I thought I'll do myself a favour and name my company after my own surname. I named the company with pride, obviously, because of the surname and where I came from.

I have considered cutting my hair off. To tell you the truth, if I cut my hair today, by the end of the year I'll be making at least three times more money than I make with dreadlocks. It is a business risk to have dreadlocks in an industry where people who are driving it don't have dreadlocks. I'm a young man and I have persevered way further than people with or without dreadlocks, because I push hard at what I do. I force matters. I make sure that you will listen to me, even if you don't want to listen. At the end of the day I have got ways that I will get business out of a company.

Since 1994 getting work has become easier for black people. It has opened up doors. Your destiny is in your own hands. Jo'burg is the place to be, in terms of the economy, but where I come from there is still real poverty. People go to bed without having a single meal. A lot of people are still suffering. But it is easier for black people to become successful business-wise. The only problem is the power struggle between different black groups. I don't see South Africa becoming anywhere close to what is happening in Zimbabwe at the moment, whereby there won't be any rule of law. I am optimistic about South Africa. I've kept all my money in South Africa. I think there's a great future here.
Motamane Mathosi ::

< Farewell party in Brixton, Johannesburg, for someone who is moving to Cape Town.

∧ A game of rough-and-tumble with the dog ended up in the pool.

In the past five years Steve Biko's Black Consciousness has been very evident. The fashion is more ethnic chic.

> **Millicent Maroga** (20) lives in Johannesburg. She is going to study at the University of Manchester on a Nelson Mandela scholarship. She is also a member of the Brightest Young Minds.

I'm originally from the East Rand, from Daveyton, a township on the east side of Johannesburg. My home language is North Sotho but I grew up speaking a variety of languages. I speak six or seven South African languages including Zulu and Xhosa. I can understand a little bit of Afrikaans but I can't speak it. I came to Jo'burg in 1999 when I was doing my first year at university. My junior degree was BA Humanities, then my Honours degree was in Industrial Sociology.

I'm going to do my MA at the University of Manchester in the UK on a Nelson Mandela scholarship; I applied for it towards the end of my Honours. The scholarship is for learners from previously disadvantaged communities. The focus is particularly on developing leadership, so people who have leadership abilities will get the scholarship. So, if you get it, you go to UK for a year. You do an MA, MBA or your PhD, but it's usually for MA students. Then you come back to South Africa and you have to give back to the country. When I applied, we had close to 13 000 applications in my year, and they took twenty students.

My parents couldn't afford to send me to university. In my matric year we were like a hundred and fifty students in my class, and only two went to university or continued with their studies.

When I went to university I was fairly young and one of the challenges I came across was the class differences between me and other black learners. Partly because RAU [Rand Afrikaans University] has always been classified as a middle-class university. Most of the black students you get there come from private schools or they live in posh suburbs. So that whole class compromise comes into the picture. The accent, the way you talk, the way you pronounce your words, it automatically tells where you're from. For the first time I experienced class segregation amongst the black students and the white students. With the white students there would be a racial issues but it wasn't an evident segregation or racism. The racism was there but it was very subtle. But amongst the black students the class differences were very obvious. The township kids would usually separate themselves. Then you have the kids from Sandton and the private schools hanging on their own, pronouncing words in a different way or talking in a different way. We called them the bourgeoisie. The word bourgeoisie in this country has been taken into township slang. People will call the way you dress bourgeois.

How did you experience the change from apartheid to democracy? I wouldn't have gone to the Rand Afrikaans University under apartheid. And I think I wouldn't have had some of the opportunities that have been availed to me, like the scholarship, getting a job. I'm a member of the Brightest Young Minds. It's a new initiative started by the University of Stellenbosch, which is also an Afrikaans university. The Brightest Young Minds is an initiative which takes place every year. They take a hundred students all over South Africa's higher institutions of education. Companies sponsor it; they come together and give you problems; they build your leadership and business skills. We get orientation to the business world and corporate world. It happens within a period of a week. I don't I think, before 1994, I would have belonged to this elite group. I'm also a member of the Golden Key Society, which is international.

In the past five years the whole notion of Steve Biko's saying 'black is beautiful' has been very evident, even though people they're not calling it the Black Consciousness Movement. Their sense of dressing has changed, they're embracing short hair and the fashion is more ethnic chic. The whole African trademark look of African girls having hips and bums, nowadays people don't have problems with it; they accept it and they're proud of it. Ten years ago people would just die if they had hips and everything. I'm not sure if it's the J-Lo [Jennifer Lopez] influence or if it is part of the whole re-emergence of the Black Consciousness Movement.

When I come back from the UK my idea is to spend five years in a corporate environment especially marketing and public relations. In 2010 I want to open my own small media enterprise, consulting, marketing and public relations.

Millicent Maroga ::

^ Carfax Club in the Newtown Precinct, downtown Johannesburg.

> At a concert in The Lounge, in Cape Town's city centre.

We are living at a stage where people have so much opportunity and kids like me are all part of the dream.

> **Leslie Kasumbu** (23) is a DJ at Yfm Radio in Johannesburg. She was born in Uganda.

Your school is obviously the place where your friends come from. My dad is a doctor and we were treated differently because we were foreigners. So I got discrimination from that, but it came more from black South Africans than it did from white South Africans, because I didn't speak a black language. When I was growing up, ninety percent of my friends were white, the other ten percent were cousins. I can remember only having a black friend when I got to high school and that was post-apartheid so to speak.

Actually I'm a singer. I'm a musician – that's what I want to do – I wanted to go into music, but, my Dad was like, 'No, no, you can't do music! You can't do music. Do something serious.' We did not speak for a long time and eventually I went to drama school. When I applied for it, he said, 'As long as you get a university degree', because in Uganda you need a degree; otherwise you are not a real person. So I went and did my whole degree and everything. But my drama school was clashing with my music and I realised I would have to make extra money to pay for my music, my piano and voice training and all the rest. And I said, 'Right! Now I need a plan.' So I'm in the canteen one day and somebody is playing this nice music and I'm thinking, 'What is going on?' I'm with my friend and she's going, 'It's just the campus radio'. And I'm, 'There's a campus radio station?' So we go upstairs and I walked in and there's this beautiful man, Cooper, and I'm standing there. I'm normally shy, and I'm like, 'Hi! I bet you I can do that better than you.' He looks up and he says, 'Excuse me? Pull up a chair.' And my friend is looking at me, like this guy is the most popular guy on campus, but I didn't know. Anyway we sit there and we do the show together. I missed my lectures and the guy said, 'This worked out cool. Come back next week.' They said if I want to stay on campus radio station I would have to pay my registration fee for campus station. Sometimes, when money was tight, I'd do anything to get near Cooper – that's all I was thinking. Anything to get near this guy – so I pay my registration and go back the second week.

The next week I go back, but he is not there, cause the idiot did something wrong and he got suspended. And here I am, stuck with the show. I'm sitting there thinking, 'What am I going to do?' That's how I got stuck in radio. I wish I had good reasons, like it was my dream, but it wasn't. But if that guy ever knew ... I promise you, it was because of you. And I liked you and you got suspended.

What is the youth culture like in Jo'burg and in South Africa? First of all the Jo'burg youth culture, and the people who are part of the Yfm, is very dynamic because they all live in the dream – like this dream Nelson Mandela had – and all of these kids like now me, between sixteen and thirty, they are all part of the dream. We are living at a stage where people have so much opportunity in South Africa and the young kids know this. They have opportunities to integrate like they never had before. It is not even an issue any more. They have opportunities to start their own businesses, which is what's happening. Everybody is doing hundreds of things. Everybody is trying to make their mark and I think the youth is going to make South Africa a world power.

And do you try to encourage the listeners, the youth, to get started now? In content we make sure that we interview people that are going to leave the youth with something positive. It is the way how you interview people. Yesterday we interviewed Isaac Chokwe – he had a TV show called *Big World*. He used to travel around the world to introduce young kids in South Africa to other cultures through him. He was like the creative director, the presenter, the producer, and Isaac is now maybe twenty-six and *Big World* is about eight years old. He put that whole show together. He's got a new show now which is about democracy, where he gets young people involved. He goes to politicians and he speaks to them. He is also one of the biggest hip-hop artists here. When we interviewed him we highlighted that, because there are kids who look up to Isaac. They don't know how hard he's worked to get where he is and that he's very dynamic. It's about the content you bring on, opposed to the people. You have to screen it.

Leslie Kasumbu ::

< Lola's Café in Long Street, Cape Town, is a popular tourist hang-out.

> Mmakau, a small village north of Pretoria.

a Paraffin Stove,
R19-95
Snowflake,
12.5 Kg
R 46-95
Selati
WHITE SUGAR
Selati White Sugar
2.5 Kg
R12-95
12.5 KG
R32-95
R10-95
Cooking
2 LT
Astor
RICE
Astor
Rice 10Kg

I was able to attend a whites-only institution, as there was no other place where I could study.

My parents were both teachers. My mother was teaching at a Catholic school. For my low primary and my primary school, I attended a Catholic school. Then in 1978, when I finished my primary school, I had to go to a high school. I only studied one year in a township school, but in 1980 it was the beginning of the schools boycott in the townships. At that time, the boycotts and everything were only happening inside the townships, not outside. People outside the townships didn't even know what was happening. Whatever they knew was what the government wanted them to know. It was all part of the propaganda system. Everything was controlled by the government. That is why the most of the white South Africans didn't even know what was happening then. Even now they don't know because of the propaganda of the past. Because of the boycotts in the 1980s we only attended school for six months. Then my mother one day came back from school and she asked me if I would be interested in going to a school in town. I said, 'Well, hmm, you know.' I never dreamed that I'd ever attend a school in town and she never ever told me about it before, that I could do that. I had to go for an interview.

It was later that I discovered that my mother spoke to a Catholic priest who recommended that I should attend school at a Christian college in Green Point. When they applied for me, they said I wanted to become a Catholic priest. Now I was able to attend that institution, a whites-only institution, as there was no other place were I could go and study. So, around Cape Town, it was very difficult; there were no institutions where blacks could study to become a Catholic priest. It had become easier after the riots in 1976. There were a lot of changes to apartheid. It wasn't just one incident that took the apartheid. There were so many changes and reforms, because the government had to look for collaborators. It means that you took certain people from the black community to be closer to you, so that apartheid could work. Those people could also bring the information about what was happening in the townships. That included informers and spies, but that was not what I was involved in.

From the 1980s on the government decided that they should get some collaborators within the apartheid system. One of the things they did was they allowed the blacks for the first time to buy houses in the cities. Now, as you saw as we were driving to my place, there were big houses on the left-hand side. So most people then were able for the first time to buy these houses. That was part of the reform.

Another reform that took place was the Tricameral Parliament, which allowed the coloureds and the Indians to vote. Now you might say it was a very good thing that happened. No, it was not good, because in voting they had to build a separate parliament for those two groups, but those two groups did not have any final say. It was still a white government that had the say in that parliament. That is what they called reforms to apartheid.

So all those things then fell under these reforms, where certain people were allowed maybe to break the law of apartheid in attending schools which before they were not allowed to attend. I was one of the first black persons who were allowed to attend a white school in town. But I didn't spy on my people; it was just for the education.
Sindile Mvambi ::

Sindile Mvambi (33) lives in a single-family home in Guguletu, Cape Town. He earns his living as a township guide.

A classroom in Observatory Junior School, Cape Town.

Sometimes we might not meet face to face, but we might through the media, and even then I'm able to complete the circuit, to draw their attention to their own legacy.

My family comes from Chatsworth in Durban, which is the largest Indian township in South Africa. It was also the first port of call for Indian people who came to this country. My great-grandparents came to South Africa from India as indentured labourers. It was all part of the colonialist slave trade. They jumped onto the ship in India, and headed for South Africa in search of a land of milk and honey.

The first time anyone ever called me a South African was when I was in Germany, and it came as a shock to me, because up to that point my self-identity was that of an Indian or Asian. Any time you filled out a form at school, anything that had to do with the population census, it would ask if you were black, white, Indian or coloured. At times it would just say 'Asian', and that was confusing, cause you'd ask your parents, 'What's Asian?' It's not even Indian. I'm not from Asia and I'm not from India. I'm from South Africa, so why didn't they write 'South African'? But that was long before apartheid was turned on its head. So I went to Germany as a Rotary exchange student in '92 as an eighteen-year-old. It was two years before the election, and Madiba had just been released from prison, and of course Europeans were hearing all this good news about South Africa. They wanted to know so much about black people and 'how does it feel to be free?' I had my little album filled with pictures of my home, and it only had pictures of Indian people in it! So there we were in Germany, and they wanted to know how black people live. And I just said, 'I don't know.'

When I came back from Germany, I went to university. In the residence on campus suddenly everybody was using the same dishes, and I thought, 'I must phone my mother and tell her we're all using the same dishes! They're not giving us separate dishes!' It was such an eye-opener. Back home we had a cupboard outside where we kept the cups and plates with chips in them that we didn't use any more. That is what we'd use when black beggars came to the house, and we'd tell them, 'Keep it. It's a gift.' We didn't want it back. Our maid would wash our dishes and clothes and make our beds, but she wasn't allowed to use our dishes. When she ate, she'd have to use the chipped dishes outside or ones that were kept under the sink. Even as a child this didn't seem normal to me. At university we would all use the same showers and toilets,

< **Nadine Naidoo** (30) is a singer, soap opera star, presenter of the show *Spirit Sundae* and founder of the organisation VIA Africa, where volunteers from all over the world get connected to organisations in South Africa.

When people ask, 'Where do you come from and what is your country like?' I know who I represent and I know who I am.

and our blankets would all be washed together, so I could end up with someone else's blanket.

In '95 the censorship laws were erased, and it was actually the pornography on campus – I was a Pharmacy student – that got me involved with Social Studies and with the students from the other parts of campus. We formed this committee and decided we were going to boycott all the stores that were degrading women in that way.

So I got to understand what black people were going through, because I talked to my girlfriends and my female lecturers, and they said, 'You think this is bad?' I said, 'This is shocking.' They said, 'In a township, before a child is six or seven years old, the child knows what sex is. The child has seen some level of sexual activity. Do you know what our houses look like? Our houses are matchboxes.' If the child wasn't exposed to it in the house, then it's the shebeens [informal bars], the bars, and the videos that get played there.

I moved from Grahamstown back to Durban and I started studying Education and Media as two separate degrees, and the Arts. So I was doing all three at the same time. And I was working also, because there was this big hunger. I wasn't clear at first about how this vision was going to take shape. I just knew I wasn't meant to be healing people on a body level.

This vision was spurred because of the need to create the change, and that by using media we could reach the most number of people all at one time. When I changed studying to a degree in Communication Science and Industrial Psychology, and the HDE in Education, and the teaching diploma in Speech and Drama through Trinity, London, I just saw them as tools. It was a multi-disciplinary approach to learning, but I only wanted to learn what I needed in order to serve.

In '98, when I realised that there were dead ends in Durban with regard to the media, I moved to Johannesburg. By now I was also understanding that to reach different people you needed to use different media. So through a children's programme I could reach the child audience; through my music I could reach people going to a music concert; through the drama series I was able to reach adults who were interested in the soap opera; through the spirituality show I'm able to reach people who were looking for those answers. As a director I'm able to reach the volunteers who don't have a voice, and who can't get onto TV. As a director/producer, I'm going to find them and say, 'Here's your platform. This is your space.' So this decade, when I was twenty to thirty, was my decade of inner transition. It might have been a national transition from apartheid to freedom, but inside of me I went through a personal transition from apartheid to freedom.

The girl that left South Africa to go to Germany back then is not the girl that leaves the country now. When I go abroad now as an ambassador and as an activist, it's with a totally different self-identity. When people ask today, 'Where do you come from and what is your country like?' I know who I represent and I know who I am.

VIA Africa has grown in the last four years from an idea to a national multimedia campaign supporting this social movement, this social activism through service. Now, with volunteering, we're able to enter each other's lives in a constructive manner. We're not being tourists of each other's lives. We're entering each other's communities to say, 'How do *you* live?' 'How can I be a part of your life?' 'How can you be a part of my life?' And so you're starting to find that people are learning more about each other. Many people say that they're actually getting more out of the volunteering experience than they're putting in. They are learning things about other cultures that they could never otherwise get; it's a treasured experience. Volunteering is deepening democracy, because it's enabling people to turn phrases in the constitution into practical living experiences.

Every person that comes to me – whether they are watching me on TV, or listening to me on the radio, or reading an article, or logging onto the website, or buying a CD – every one of these mediums is a connection between my spirit and that person's spirit. Sometimes we might not meet face to face, but we might through the media, and even then I'm able to complete the circuit, to draw their attention to their own legacy.

Nadine Naidoo ::

^ Nadine during her show *Spirit Sundae*, in the SABC studios, Johannesburg.

>> A boy playing in Kliptown, Soweto, Johannesburg (pages 152–153).